ISBN 978-1-331-98274-6
PIBN 10054704

This book is a reproduction of an important historical work. Forgotten Books uses state-of-the-art technology to digitally reconstruct the work, preserving the original format whilst repairing imperfections present in the aged copy. In rare cases, an imperfection in the original, such as a blemish or missing page, may be replicated in our edition. We do, however, repair the vast majority of imperfections successfully; any imperfections that remain are intentionally left to preserve the state of such historical works.

For support please visit www.forgottenbooks.com

1 MONTH OF
FREE
READING

at

www.ForgottenBooks.com

By purchasing this book you are eligible for one month membership to ForgottenBooks.com, giving you unlimited access to our entire collection of over 700,000 titles via our web site and mobile apps.

To claim your free month visit:

www.forgottenbooks.com/free54704

English
Français
Deutsche
Italiano
Español
Português

www.forgottenbooks.com

Mythology Photography **Fiction**
Fishing Christianity **Art** Cooking
Essays Buddhism Freemasonry
Medicine **Biology** Music **Ancient
Egypt** Evolution Carpentry Physics
Dance Geology **Mathematics** Fitness
Shakespeare **Folklore** Yoga Marketing
Confidence Immortality Biographies
Poetry **Psychology** Witchcraft
Electronics Chemistry History **Law**
Accounting **Philosophy** Anthropology
Alchemy Drama Quantum Mechanics
Atheism Sexual Health **Ancient History**
Entrepreneurship Languages Sport
Paleontology Needlework Islam
Metaphysics Investment Archaeology
Parenting Statistics Criminology
Motivational

HANDBOOKS OF PRACTICAL GARDENING
EDITED BY HARRY ROBERTS

THE BOOK OF THE PANSY, VIOLA
AND VIOLET

AN ARRANGEMENT OF RAYLESS YELLOW TUFTED PANSIES OR VIOLAS FOR DECORATIVE EFFECT

BY

"Frolic virgins once there were,
　Over-loving, living here
　Being here their ends denied,
　Ran for sweethearts mad, and died.
　Love, in pity of their tears,
　And their loss in blooming years,
　For their restless here-spent hours,
　Gave them Heart's-ease turned to flowers.
　　　　　　　　　　—HERRICK.

NEW YORK : JOHN LANE COMPANY. MCMVIII

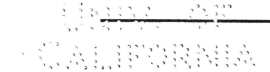

Turnbull & Spears, Printers, Edinburgh

CONTENTS

CHAP.   PAGE

 I. THE PANSY. Introduction   1

 II. PANSIES. Show and Fancy Types and Continental
   Strains 7

 III. TUFTED PANSIES OR VIOLAS. Various types 11

 IV. PROPAGATION. Propagation by seed—By cuttings—By
   division of old plants 18

 V. PLANTING OUT IN BEDS AND BORDERS, &c. Soils—Preparation of soil in beds and borders—Planting—Planting
   in frames with a view to an early display—Culture
   in Pots—Tufted Pansies and Violettas in pans and
   baskets 36

 VI. GENERAL CULTIVATION OF THE PANSY VIOLA AND VIOLETTA,
   AND TREATMENT WHEN GROWN FOR EXHIBITION . 51

 VII. EXHIBITING. Pansy tray—Sprays—Bowls—Pans 57

 VIII. THE USE OF PANSIES AS CUT FLOWERS FOR HOUSE DECORATION 62

 IX. PANSIES IN THE FLOWER GARDEN AND HARDY BORDER 64

 X. VIOLETTAS OR MINIATURE TUFTED PANSIES . 67

 XI. RAISING NEW VARIETIES FROM SEED AND METHOD OF CROSSING
   —Sports 72

 XII. SELECTIONS OF BEST VARIETIES. Show Pansies—Fancy
   Pansies—Tufted Pansies or Violas—Violettas 76

VIOLETS

 XIII. THE VIOLET. Introduction—Wild Varieties 86

 XIV. SWEET VIOLETS. Soil—Position—Growing in frames—
   Propagation and planting out—General cultivation
   during Summer—Propagation by seed—Pot Culture 94

 XV. SELECTIONS. Single Violets—Double Violets 102

  INDEX 105

253056

LIST OF ILLUSTRATIONS

AN ARRANGEMENT OF RAYLESS YELLOW TUFTED PANSIES OR VIOLAS FOR DECORATIVE EFFECT . *Frontispiece*
  (*From a photo by J. W. Parker*)

TO FACE PAGE

DIFFERENT TYPES OF SHOW PANSIES—1. DARK SELF; 2. WHITE OR YELLOW SELF; 3. YELLOW GROUND; 4. WHITE GROUND 8
  (*Reprinted by kind permission of Messrs Dobbie, of Rothesay, from " Pansies, Violas and Violets "*)

A TYPE OF A YELLOW SELF VIOLA (VERY SLIGHTLY RAYED) 10
  (*From a photo by J. W. Parker*)

A TYPE OF A DARK SELF VIOLA 12

FANCY TYPE OF THE VIOLA (SOMETIMES KNOWN AS THE "COUNTESS OF KINTORE" TYPE 14

ANOTHER OF THE FANCY TYPE OF VIOLA. "THE MEARNS" 16

EDGED TYPE OF FLOWER. VIOLA "DUCHESS OF FIFE" . 18
  (*Reprinted by kind permission of Messrs Dobbie, of Rothesay, from " Pansies, Violas and Violets "*)

ANOTHER TYPE OF AN EDGED VIOLA. THE MARGIN IN THIS CASE IS BROADER AND MORE REGULARLY DEFINED 20

STRIPED TYPE OF VIOLA 22

A RAYED TYPE OF THE TUFTED PANSY OR VIOLA 24

RAYLESS TYPE OF VIOLA 26
  (*The above are reproduced by kind permission of Messrs Dobbie, of Rothesay, from " Pansies, Violas and Violets "*)

VIOLA "LARK." SLIGHTLY EDGED HELIOTROPE BLUE 28
  (*From a photo by J. W. Parker*)

TO FACE PAGE

AN IDEAL TYPE OF CUTTING, PROPERLY TRIMMED. THIS SHOULD BE CUT IMMEDIATELY BELOW THE JOINT, AS MARKED BY THE DOTTED LINE 30

YOUNG GROWTH DETACHED WITH ROOTLETS ADHERING. A SURE AND EASY MEANS OF INCREASING STOCK . 32

HOLLOW GROWTH OR STEM CUTTING. USELESS FOR PROPAGATING PURPOSES 34

VIOLA TUFT IN BORDER 42
(By courtesy of Mr W. Sydenham of Tamworth)

TUFTED PANSY OR VIOLA "GREY FRIAR" . . . 50
(From a photo by J. W. Parker)

IMPROVED PANSY STAND 58

VIOLA "PRIMROSE DAME." BLOOMS ARRANGED IN A SAUCER FOR TABLE DECORATION, ETC. 62
(From a photo by J. W. Parker)

A SMALL BOWL OF VIOLETTA, "QUEEN OF THE YEAR" 68

VIOLA "HARRY BAMBER" 74
(From a photo by J. W. Parker)

A PLANT OF A TUFTED PANSY IN FULL BLOOM, AFTER A SEASON'S GROWTH 80
(By courtesy of Mr W. Sydenham of Tamworth)

AN EXHIBIT OF VIOLET BLOOMS 90

PLANTING VIOLETS FOR MARKET AT MESSRS ISAAC HOUSE'S NURSERIES, WESTBURY-ON-TRYM 98

THE BOOK OF THE PANSY, VIOLA
AND VIOLET

THE BOOK OF THE PANSY, VIOLA AND VIOLET

CHAPTER I

THE PANSY

INTRODUCTION

THE beautiful flowers of the Pansy, that we are now accustomed to see in nearly every garden worthy of the name, were not evolved in one short space of time. They are the outcome of many years of persistent effort on the part of a comparatively few enthusiasts, who, by dint of infinite patience and labour, have helped to evolve the glorious blooms that are now so largely grown.

The origin of the Pansy is, to a certain extent, wrapt in obscurity. The earliest detailed information we have of any special work being done with the Pansy, is that of Lord Gambier and his gardener, Thompson by name. These two pioneers conducted their experiments at Iver in Buckinghamshire at the beginning of last century, 1813 to wit.

They first began experimenting with the common *Viola tricolor* or Heart's-ease, and encouraged by their success in this direction, widened their field of operations by working on other species. We cannot do better than quote Thompson's own words, when writing in the Flower Gardener's Library and Floricultural Cabinet in the year 1841, which, most happily, have been preserved to us.

" About seven or eight and twenty years ago, Lord

Gambier brought me a few roots of the common yellow and white Heart's-ease, which he had gathered in the grounds at Iver, and requested that I would cultivate them. Always eager to please my worthy and ever-to-be-lamented master I did so, sowed the seed, and found that they improved far beyond my most sanguine expectations. In consequence thereof, I collected all the varieties that could be obtained. From Brown of Slough I had the blue; and from some other person, whose name I do not now recollect, a darker sort, said to have been imported from Russia. These additions wonderfully improved my breeders. But still, though the varieties I soon obtained were multitudinous, their size was almost as diminutive as the originals. Nevertheless his lordship was pleased, and thus I was amply rewarded. Up to this period, which was about four years after my commencement, I began imperceptibly to grow pleased with the pursuit, for all who saw my collection declared themselves delighted therewith. I then began to think that some of my sorts were worthy of propagation; and this circumstance led me to give one, which took his lordship's fancy, a name. This was entitled Lady Gambier, and as I struck cuttings of it, they were given as presents by my worthy employers to their numerous friends and acquaintances. The character of this flower was so very similar to that which was afterwards spread about under the name of George the Fourth, that I have no doubt but that variety was a seed therefrom. Who raised it I could never ascertain. This, though in comparison with the worst flower now grown, and many even of the named varieties are still bad enough, would even beside them be reckoned little better than a weed. Still, Lady Gambier was the beauty of her tribe, and won golden opinions from every beholder. It was, indeed, in shape little more symmetrical than a child's windmill, but looked in size among the sisterhood like a giant surrounded by dwarfs. But the giant of those days would be a pigmy now, as Lady Gambier herself appeared in comparison with another flower, which I soon after raised ; and which, on account of what I then considered its monstrous proportions, I christened Ajax. This, I then thought, could never be surpassed, and yet in shape it was as lengthy as a horse's head. Still I had worked wonders, and I resolved to persevere. I did so, and was at length rewarded by producing rich colouring, large size, and fine shape. The first large and good-shaped flower that I raised was named Thompson's King. Still, up to this period, a dark eye, which is now considered one of the chief requisites in a first-rate flower, had never been seen. Indeed such a feature had never entered my imagination, nor can I take any merit to myself for originating this peculiar property, for it was entirely the offspring of chance. In looking one morning over a collection of heaths, which had been some time neglected, I was struck, to use a vulgar expression, all of a heap, by seeing what appeared to me a miniature cat's face steadfastly gazing at me. It was the flower of a Heart's-ease, self-sown, and hitherto left to waste its beauty far from mortal's eye. I immediately took it up and gave it a local habitation and a name! This first child of the tribe I called Madoro, and from her bosom came the seed which, after various generations, produced Victoria, who in her turn became the mother of many even more beautiful than herself. Hitherto in the way of colour nothing new had been introduced ; white, yellow, and blue in their numerous shades seemed to be the only colours which the Heart's-ease was capable of throwing out, till about four years since, when I discovered in my seedling-bed a dark-bronze flower, which I immediately marked and baptised Flamium—from which have sprung Tarton, Vivid, and the King of Beauties, which only bloomed this Spring, and is decidedly the best flower of its kind that has ever been submitted to public inspection."

From this time forth, by patience and application, the Pansy in its various forms was slowly but surely evolved, until the present time when we possess an infinite number of varieties of almost all shades of colour, from the pure white of the Tufted Pansy (Viola) to the purple and crimson colours of the Fancy Pansy. In fact we may say all the colours of the spectrum, with the exception of green, are represented. There have been several black varieties, but these have been superseded, as is well, their only recommendation being that of novelty. So far as we have been able to ascertain, no green variety has yet been raised, but even if it ever is, it will have no use in the garden, but can only be regarded as a monstrosity.

As there seems to be a great amount of uncertainty in the minds of many people as to the difference between the various types of the Pansy, perhaps it would be well to quote a passage from " the Garden" of 16th January 1892, which should clear up any doubt or difficulty which may have arisen in the mind of the reader. Speaking of the Tufted Pansy (commonly known as the Viola) it says :—

" These are hybrids of Pansies and Alpine Violets. The term 'tufted' has been very properly used to distinguish plants of a spreading habit, like Pinks, Aubretia and Alpine Violets, from plants with single erect stems like, say, the Stock, Lupine, and Aster. Sometimes the two forms of habit occur in the same family; for instance, there are Violas that are tufted and Violas that are not—the German, French, and other Pansies in our gardens do not spread at the root as the Tufted Pansies do. Plants of this 'tufted' habit are often a mass of delicate rootlets even above the ground, so that they are easily increased. Hence when older Pansies die after flowering, those crossed with the Alpine species remain like true perennials, and are easily increased. The term 'Pansies' is a good one in all ways. Without an English name, we shall always have confusion with the Latin name for the name of the wild species. To all of these belongs the old Latin name of the genus *Viola*. It is now agreed by botanists that all cross-bred garden plants— including Tufted Pansies, of course—should have popular English not Latin names. 'Bedding Viola' is a vulgar compound of bad English and bad Latin; whereas 'Tufted Pansies' is a good English name with a clear meaning."

To help us still further to classify them more easily, we will read what the late Dr Stuart—who did so much for the Tufted Pansy—says :—

" Botanically, Violets, Pansies and Heart's-ease are all the same. Tufted Pansies are crosses from the Garden Pansy and *Viola cornuta*, the latter being the seed-bearer. Pollen from *Viola cornuta* applied to the Pansy produces a common enough form of bedding Pansy—never the tufted root growth obtained when the cross is the other way. I have proved this by actual hand-crossing. Most strains of Tufted Pansies are bred the wrong way, and in consequence lack the fibrous tufted root which makes the Violetta strain perennial."

Some contend that the Pansy is the result of con-tinuous selection of seedlings from *Viola tricolor*, whilst others maintain that the result was arrived at by the intercrossing of *V. tricolor*, *V. cornuta*, *V. altaica*, *V. lutea* and *V. grandiflora*. In all probability the Pansies and Violas we now grow are really the outcome of the use of all the above-mentioned species.

Professor Hillhouse gave some interesting notes in a paper, which he read before the Viola Conference in 1895, and which may not be out of place to quote here. He points out that " the natural results of insect fertilisation, should species be grown together which are capable of interaction, is to produce what, for want of a better expression, we will call *natural hybrids*; and it is by no means impossible that the cultivated Pansies of the early part of this century had their origin in some such fashion as this, and that such a Botanical Garden as that of Paris might well enough have given existence to one at least of the garden races. In this, as in so many cases, historical evidence is valueless on account of its vagueness, and there are but three courses open to one who wishes to work at such a question as this. One is to institute careful morphological anatomical comparisons between the result and its supposed parents; another is to work backwards, and, as the modern plant has presumably been produced by a synthesis, so to try and resolve its parentage by an analysis—to select, that is, various seedlings as widely removed from the cultivated form as possible, and so with their seedlings in their turn, and thus bring into play the scientific principle involved in that limited tendency to ' reversion' which all cultivated plants possess. The third method is to endeavour to build up the Pansy again, as indeed M. Carrière is said to have done, and to have thus produced from the wild *V. tricolor* (whatever that may be) flowers very like those of the cultivated Pansy."

From these extracts, it will be seen that from Lord Gambier and his co-pioneers we have had handed ‚down to us the garden Pansy—and from this, other workers have produced the Tufted Pansy (Viola), by means of cross fertilisation and selection, etc.

We think, therefore, that the simplest plan will be to classify the various types under five heads as follows :—

Show Pansy—Fancy Pansy—Continental Strains—Tufted Pansy—Violettas (miniature flowered Tufted Pansies).

CHAPTER II

ALTHOUGH the number of Pansies grown promiscuously is legion, and these of all shades and colours, two sections only are recognised as suitable for high cultivation. On the one hand, we have the Show Pansy or English kinds, and on the other we have the Fancy or Belgian kinds. Any doubt as to the distinction between the two kinds is very easily disposed of, as it is merely practically the difference between the markings or blotches of the flowers. Contrasting the two divisions we have :—

SHOW PANSY

These are subdivided into two divisions, namely: *Belted Pansies*—white and yellow grounds ; *Selfs*—white, yellow and dark colours. In form, the blooms should be practically circular, smooth, and with no sign of waviness in the petals.

In texture, stoutness of the petals is a *sine qua non*, and they should possess that velvety appearance and glossiness, which has attracted so many people to these flowers.

Three rules are to be observed in colour and markings. The three lower petals should be of exactly the same colour, whatever the ground colour may happen to be. The two top petals, also, should be of the same tint as that of the belting round the edge of the other three, and this belting should be clear cut and well defined, and should be uniform in width throughout. There should be no suffusion whatever from the belt into the ground colour.

As to the blotch, this should be uniform in shade, dense and solid, and circular, so far as possible, in shape.

The colour of the eye should be of a bright orange tint, with no rays running into it, clear cut, and well defined.

The size of the bloom ought not to be less than 2 inches in diameter; at any rate for competition.

In the selfs, which should be of decided colours, there should be uniformity throughout. They should possess a neat eye with a dark, dense blotch, as clear cut and well defined as is possible. The main point is to get a good contrast between the blotch and the ground colour.

Fancy Pansy

In this section the main idea is to have the blotch as large as possible, covering most of the surface of the three lower petals. As follows :—

In form, the bloom should be as circular as far as can be, the petals, which should be thick and velvety in texture, lying flat and smooth with as little sign of waviness as possible.

The colours of the Fancy Pansy are not, like the Show Pansy, narrowed down within well-defined limits.

The blotch, which should be dense and solid, should occupy the whole surface of the three lower petals, with the exception of a narrow belt or margin, which it may flush into. The belting may be either all one colour or several colours, and the top petals may be of any shade of colour whatever.

The bloom should possess a good neat eye of a bright orange colour with no sign of rays.

DIFFERENT TYPES OF SHOW PANSIES

1. DARK SELF
2. WHITE OR YELLOW SELF
3. YELLOW GROUND
4 WHITE GROUND

Reprinted by kind permission of Messrs. Dobbie, of Rothesay, from " Pansies, Violas, and Violets '

So beautiful and varied are the newer flowers of the Fancy Pansy, that they are beyond the imagination of many people who only grow the commoner sorts, and who are missing what may be aptly described as "a thing of beauty and a joy for ever."

Both Show and Fancy Pansies have many traits in common as regards their shape and form. In both, the bottom petal should be of about half the size of the whole flower, and its top edge should be as near as possible horizontal, with no sign of sloping. The two petals immediately above it should be of a size sufficient to meet above the eye. All the petals should be of a good stout texture so as not to present a "floppy" appearance. This, of course, applies more to the two top petals, which, if of an insufficient strength in texture, have a natural tendency to droop. Particularly may this be noticed in exceedingly large flowers, the texture of which is not strong enough to bear the extra weight put upon them, owing to the fact of their being so large.

The feature that gives to such a large degree that *finesse* which should be so earnestly sought after, is the eye and its setting. This should be of medium size, neither too large or too small. If the eye is too small, the flower loses that imposing appearance which is a great desideratum, and if too large the bloom shows want of refinement.

The brows of the eye should be of a light shade of colour, thus creating a good contrast.

Of course, if all these rules were strictly and rigidly adhered to, a great many of our prettier varieties would consequently be excluded, which would be a great pity indeed; but the foregoing rules help to show the ideal to which specialists and others are working.

Many are the improvements which can still be made in the Pansy, and a wide field is open to the earnest and patient amateur (in the original sense of the word) in which to bring the flower to that pitch of perfection which always seems unattainable, however nearly it is approached.

CONTINENTAL STRAINS

In addition to the Show and the Fancy Pansies there are numerous continental strains largely grown, two of the best known being Bugnot's and the Trimadeau Pansy.

Plants of this description are raised in immense quantities by Market Growers, who make quite a speciality of this department of their business. Not seldom their Nursery Grounds are situated in favourable quarters, where under fairly hardy conditions good plants can be turned out in the early Spring. At this time they are sent to Market neatly done up, and sold in boxes of about two dozen in each, at a low figure, and at a price that the retailers by whom they are distributed are enabled to offer them to purchasers at a compaiatively cheap rate. Hence the reason for the remarkable display sometimes seen in Costermongers' barrows, which seldom fails to attract buyers. Many florists and others, in and around large towns, also find a ready market for these Pansies of continental origin. As a rule, the plants grow well until about the end of June, when, with the approach of really warm weather, they succumb to the peculiarities of our English climate at that period. They lack constitution, however; and this is another reason why the named varieties of English and Scotch florists, which possess such a great advantage over the Continental kinds, are to be preferred.

These continental varieties are invariably propagated by seed, and if the seed is sown in May or June, pricked off during July, and planted out early in the Autumn, an effective display may be made with them in the late Spring and early Summer of the following year.

A TYPE OF A YELLOW SELF VIOLA (VERY **SLIGHTLY RAYED**)

CHAPTER III

TUFTED PANSIES OR VIOLAS

CHARMING and beautiful as the Show and the Fancy Pansy are, however; the Tufted Pansy (Viola) is, for general all-round utility, pre-eminently superior. Possessing, as it does, so compact a growth in comparison with the Pansy, and so hardy and robust a constitution, combined with such wonderful free-flowering propensities, and also with such remarkably diverse markings and colours, the Viola ranks second to none, when planted in masses, edgings, or for the general beautifying of the flower garden. The most pleasing and useful characteristic of the Viola is the extensive period over which it bears its flowers; the plants beginning to bloom in the early Spring, and continuing without abatement far into the Autumn. In fact, the writer has picked blooms off certain varieties of Violas on Christmas Day, and this in the open, in a by no means sheltered position. Of course the blooms were very rough ones, and of little practical value, but it just serves to illustrate the remarkable propensity this type of the Pansy has for flowering for such a length of time.

Few subjects in the hardy flower garden will give such remarkable results in return for so little trouble and expense as the Tufted Pansy. The habit, as above mentioned, when compared with that of the Pansy, is so much more compact and therefore more adaptable for bedding purposes. It is these features, together with the above-mentioned properties, which cause the Tufted

Pansy to be grown in most large gardens, and in the great parks in London and its environs, and in the large towns in the provinces.

We are fortunate, indeed, in being able to grow the Tufted Pansy with the facility and success with which it is grown in the South of England. With Show and with Fancy Pansies this is not the case, as the growing of these in the South requires the expenditure of a great deal more care and trouble. In the North, however, the conditions of climate are such as are just ideal for both Pansies and Violas; and this accounts for the immense size of the blooms shown by the Scotch specialists. From this it will be inferred that as the Viola delights in the cool bracing climate of the North, it would prefer the cooler spots in the garden. This is so, but at the same time Violas do equally well in positions in which they receive the full heat of the sun the greater part of the day. Providing they are well looked after and a good mulching given from time to time, they will flower without cessation from April to October.

The cultivation of Violas having increased by leaps and bounds during the past ten years or so, it becomes somewhat easier to define the now accepted shape and traits of the Viola than was the case, say, in the early eighties, if the characteristics of the Viola could have been defined then.

No hard and fast rule exists which decrees the shape of the Viola. In some cases we have long or oval blooms, and in other cases we have blooms of a circular shape.

There are several types of the Viola recognised, which are set down in detail hereunder.

Selfs.—In which the blooms consist of one colour only, such as white, yellow, blue. These may be represented by the three Violas—Swan, Mrs E. A. Cade, Admiral of the Blues.

TYPE OF A DARK SELF VIOLA

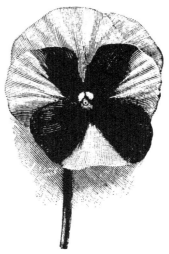

FANCY TYPE OF THE VIOLA
(SOMETIMES KNOWN AS THE
COUNTESS OF KINTORE" TYPE)

ANOTHER OF THE FANCY TYPE
OF VIOLA. "THE MEARNS"

EDGED TYPE OF FLOWER. VIOLA
"DUCHESS OF FIFE"

*Reprinted by kind permission of Messrs Dobbie, of Rothesay, from "Pansies,
Violas and Violets"*

Fancy.—This type is also very often known as the " Countess of Kintore " type, from the name of one of the most popular varieties of this particular type raised. Generally speaking, "fancies" may be described as blooms of a mauve ground, blotched with purple and black, and sometimes white, to a greater or lesser degree, as the case may be. They are exceedingly velvety and glossy in appearance. Three well-known representative sorts are — Cottage Maid, The Mearns, Mrs T. W. R. Johnstone.

Margined.—This type consists of flowers having a belt or margin of colour round the petals. In some cases the band is quite clear and well cut; in others, it is irregular. Regularity in this respect is not sought after, and, indeed, from an artistic point of view should not be desired. Typical varieties are—Goldfinch, Lady Grant, Sunbeam.

In addition to the above-mentioned types we have also striped flowers, which are to the taste of some people.

However, as above stated, there is no fixed rule as to what colour or shape a Viola bloom should be, except that of one's own judgment, which is gradually educated up to distinguishing between a poor specimen and a good one.

Unlike the Show and the Fancy Pansies there should be no blotch, as this is now considered a blemish, and is only allowed on sufferance, when the bloom or plant possesses some extraordinary properties of colour or growth. The blotch in the Viola has now been practically eliminated, and it is only in a few well-known old stagers that we see it. These, as mentioned above, have some extra charm of colour, etc., which for the time being outweighs any prejudices which may exist owing to their bad form.

Then, again, some varieties are rayed and others rayless,

The question of rays or no rays, to a great extent, is a matter for individual taste, some preferring the rayed varieties, others the rayless. It must be admitted, however, that the absence of rays creates a charm and refinement in the flower, which is totally absent if it be heavily rayed. This is especially noticeable in blooms of light shades, and selfs. There are so many beautiful rayless varieties in commerce now, that it would seem invidious to mention any particular one as being typical of the rayless form of this flower.

It is to the late Dr Chas. Stuart that we are indebted for this wonderful improvement; and for the present, suffice it to say, the rayless varieties which we now grow, and which so greatly add to the beauty and charm of our gardens, probably owe their existence to a chance seedling of Dr Stuart's, which he named " Violetta," of which more hereafter. This " Violetta " was quite rayless, and had a delightful almond perfume. Dr Stuart worked on this variety, and crossed it with a white rayed self then largely cultivated, and by this means obtained " Sylvia," a variety which up to a few years ago was seen in the garden of almost every Viola grower.

Like the parent variety it possesses a beautiful tufted habit, and a fine robust constitution, both of which are so sadly lacking in some of the newer kinds. It bears flowers in abundance, and owing to its tufted habit is well adapted for withstanding the scorching effects of hot, dry weather. Many varieties have been raised from " Sylvia," and all possessing the same hardy characteristics and tufted habit of growth. The creation of this flower undoubtedly brought new blood into the Viola, and were it not for this variety, many plants would lack the stamina and tufted root growths which they now possess, and which help to make the Viola the unqualified success it is. For, owing to crossing and intercrossing, the " Sylvia " characteristics have been incorporated in new seedlings, until now it is extremely difficult to ascertain whether they are, or are not, descendents of such a noble ancestor. Encouraged by this new success, Dr Stuart raised many others, all having the same characteristics as the parent plant. Some of the best-known are—*Blue Gown*, mauve-blue; *Florizel*, lilac blush; *Ethereal*, a beautiful heliotrope; *Rosea Pallida*, very pale rose; and many others.

Unfortunately, perhaps, for some things, the plants in the first stage of their existence—that is to say, when propagated the season previous to their being planted out— are, owing to their character of growth, somewhat small. When customers receive from the specialist these small pieces, being unaware of the possibilities lying latent within them, they are apt to be somewhat disappointed at their small size. This more especially the case when compared with some of the lanky exhibition sorts. But so soon as the above-named type of plant is estab- lished, and has started to grow, it soon begins to assert its superiority. At once it commences to make up for apparently lost time, by breaking out from underneath into innumerable little growths. These quickly increase in size, and before many weeks are over, the small piece is represented by a delightful little carpet of green, some 3 to 4 inches across, and above this is a profusion of flowers borne well above the foliage on stiff erect footstalks.

But what of the exhibition type of plant? In the majority of instances mere size of flowers is sought after at the expense of everything else. No matter how coarse the growth, how utterly unsuited for garden embellishment, how difficult to grow, or how far from a really Tufted Pansy it may depart, the one redeeming feature of size secures for it a place in the lists of specialists, and recog- nition on the stands at the shows. What is the result? The competitor who shows first-class blooms of ordinary varieties, however well grown they may be, stands but little chance amongst the titanic specimens of the coarse exhibition kinds.

The latter, unlike their small brethren, make large plants to send out, as the cuttings are always so much more lanky; and this fact leads the novice to think that the lanky and large plants are much better and more forward than the "Sylvia" or "Cornuta" type. But this, of course, is not the case. In some instances, these large varieties have early blooms which not seldom are their best, for, as the plant commences to grow and lateral growths begin to appear, the main stem gets more lanky, and at last topples over on to its side. Very few flowers are then produced, and these of poor quality, and the plant is not infrequently bereft of flowers until the shoots that are evolved at the base of the plant have grown sufficiently well to produce flowers. This stage is, perhaps, the happiest part of the existence of plants of this type, for these growths get more elongated as time proceeds, and the strength of the plant is given out in producing rank growth. The best method to adopt when this happens, is to cut off all the long growths; this will enable the plant to break away into growth again, and produce more flowers.

It will thus be seen, that although the flowers are of immense size when the plants are taken care of, there are times when great difficulty is experienced in obtaining even passable blooms. The great thing when grown for exhibition, which is in reality the only useful sphere of the type under notice, is to time the growth of the plants, so that when the show is about to take place they are in just that state to produce blooms of a quality to succeed.

The habit of this ungainly type of plant resembles the growth of the Fancy Pansy rather than that of the true "Tufted Pansy," and it may confidently be assumed by anyone that it therefore shares the likes and dislikes of the Fancy Pansy. Like this latter too, owing to its **not** possessing that fibrous root growth of the Tufted Pansy, it is not so well suited for the hot weather experienced during the summer months in the South of England.

It behoves the tyro, then, if he wishes to succeed in growing Violas well—more especially with a view to beautifying the garden—to grow only those varieties that have the tufted habit of growth, the flowers of which will beautify the garden from April to October with their charming display.

The larger-flowered varieties with their ungainly growth are all very well from an exhibition point of view, where size is the great end, but they are to be admired more as the outcome of the florist's skill than for their utility in adding to the beauty and brightness of the garden. They are not so free-flowering on the whole as the more tufted kinds, and considerable disappointment is thus often caused when they are grown for their effect in the garden.

B

CHAPTER IV

PROPAGATION

THERE are three recognised methods of propagating Pansies and Violas, viz.: by seed, by cuttings, and by breaking up or dividing old plants into small pieces with a few roots adhering.

The various methods of procedure are as follows:—

PROPAGATION BY SEED

This method of propagation is much favoured by those persons who wish for a cheap and easy way of becoming the possessors of a few plants with which to brighten the flower borders and garden generally. As a rule, they are not particular as to what sort of blooms they obtain, also as to whether they are of good form, or good bedders, or anything of that sort. They like to grow a few, just for "a bit of colour," and a very good and interesting way too.

It must be remembered that Pansies and Violas rarely come true from seed, and if stock of a certain variety is wanted, propagation will have to take place by means of cuttings taken from plants of that particular variety, or by breaking up the old plants. Only occasionally does a seedling plant come true to the parent variety, for, owing to the botanical structure of the Pansy, fertilisation by insects becomes so very easy of accomplishment.

Fertilisation by insects is clearly and distinctly described to us by Professor Hillhouse (at the Viola

18

Conference in 1895), who says: "If an insect proboscis be inserted into the spur, the insect's eye having perhaps been guided thereto by the radiating lines so common in the wilding pansies, the surface of the proboscis will be licked, so to speak, by the projecting lip, and pollen, if any, brought from a previous Pansy flower, will be left upon its viscid surface. When withdrawn, powdered with pollen from the anthers below, the flexible lip is pushed up, only its dry under surface being presented to the proboscis, and in the same action the pollen upon the upper surface of the lip is transferred to the still more viscid hollow surface of the stigma, there to develop and fertilise the ovules."

It will be seen, therefore, that if different varieties are grown in close proximity to one another, the chances are, that resulting seedlings grown from the seed saved from any of these flowers will be crosses of many different varieties.

There are several periods of the year during which seed may be sown, and to a great extent it is a matter of convenience.

Care should be taken that only the best seed is used, and for this reason it should be obtained either from a specialist or saved from the grower's own plants. The latter method is far more interesting, but if the grower has only a small selection of plants, there will not be much likelihood of a good variability in the resulting seedlings.

If the seed can be obtained from a specialist whose collection may comprise some hundreds of different varieties, this is much to be preferred. This is, of course, apart from the question of artificial hybridisation, which is dealt with in another chapter.

A sowing may be made at the end of July or beginning of August, and to this end a special compost should be prepared. Equal parts of loam and leaf soil should be taken, and to these should be added a liberal quantity of sharp sand just sufficient to make the compost porous. The ingredients should be passed through a sieve with a mesh of about half an inch, and the whole thoroughly mixed and afterwards placed in a dry situation. The question as to whether the compost is porous or not may be easily tested by taking a handful and pressing it rather tightly. If sufficient sand has been added the compost will fall away readily.

The sowing may take place almost anywhere—in pots, pans, frames, boxes, or in the open ground. For this period, perhaps, the best method is to use a small frame with a frame-light, so that the seeds may be protected from any heavy rain and from the depredations of birds, and also as a means of preventing the frame from being used as a happy hunting-ground for cats and such like. The seeds may also be sown in the greenhouse, but an outdoor position is preferable, as the small plants are apt to get infested with green fly at this period of the year in more artificial and unnatural conditions.

If a small frame is not available, the bottom of a fairly large box can be knocked out, the four remaining sides forming a frame quite suitable for the present purpose. This can be covered with a small frame-light or pieces of glass until germination takes place, thus affording protection from the elements.

Assuming the above method is to be followed, a position with a fairly warm aspect should be chosen, and the ground on which the frame is to stand should be lightly forked over, and then pressed down level and firmed with the back of a spade.

The compost, to the depth of several inches, should then be introduced, and this also levelled and made fairly firm. It is important that the surface should be quite level.

Before sowing the seeds, a light watering from a fine-rosed can should be given, and the compost, thus

ANOTHER TYPE OF AN EDGED
VIOLA. THE MARGIN IN THIS
CASE IS BROADER AND MORE
REGULARLY DEFINED

STRIPED TYPE OF VIOLA

A RAYED TYPE OF THE TUFTED
PANSY OR VIOLA

RAYLESS TYPE OF VIOLA

*The above are reproduced by kind permission of Messrs Dobbie, of Rothesay,
from " Pansies, Violets and Violas "*

moistened, should stand for some hours before the seed is sown.

The seed may be sown either in little furrows, or sown broadcast. The latter is perhaps the most popular method, but the great thing to remember is, not to sow too thickly or to allow the seed to be crowded together in some parts, and very thin in others, but to attempt to obtain an even distribution over the whole surface.

If the seed is seen to be somewhat crowded in some places, it can be distributed more evenly by means of the end of a pencil or stick, thus preventing over-crowding, which would be a certain forerunner of weakness in the young plants.

The seed being sown thus satisfactorily, a thin covering of the compost should be scattered across as evenly as possible to the depth of about a quarter of an inch or less. The whole surface should then be pressed down gently and evenly with a small board, or the back of a spade.

Then, if the sowing has been done in a frame in the manner suggested, the frame-light should be placed thereon, and this covered with mats or newspapers in order to exclude the light and act as a shield from the sun until the seeds have germinated.

The young seedlings should be carefully shaded from the heat of the mid-day sun, and if the soil begins to look dry, they should be given a gentle watering with a very fine-rosed can. As the seedlings commence to grow, they can gradually be allowed more air, and finally the frame-light may be dispensed with altogether.

During this time worms may possibly create some trouble by disturbing the soil, causing the young plants either to be engulfed in the holes thus made, or to be thrown up out of the soil altogether, thereby allowing the plant to perish. A sharp lookout should be kept for anything of this nature, and when seen, the seedlings should be pressed back into their proper position if possible. A few handfuls of sharp sand strewn upon the soil seems to be of good effect in keeping worms under. Slugs also may make an appearance at this time. These should be sought after at night or in the early morning, and an end put to their existence.

When the seedlings have developed their fourth leaf, and are of a convenient size to handle, they should be lifted with care and pricked out into more roomy quarters.

The seedling plants may be pricked out either into other frames or into the open ground. The better plan, perhaps, is. to employ the former method, as by this means protection may be given to them during the severe weather so often experienced in December and January. At the same time, however, they should on no account be coddled, but be allowed to develop into hardy and stocky little plants, and this may be achieved by the admission of air on all possible occasions. The soil in which they are to be pricked out should be of the same nature as the compost they were sown in, and this having been firmly pressed down, the following method of procedure should be adopted : A number of seedlings having been lifted, they should be carefully separated and dibbled in, some 3 to 4 inches apart. A small dibber with a flat end should be used—a stick about 6 to 8 inches long and $\frac{3}{4}$ inch in diameter, having one end well pared down flat, makes a capital instrument —and this should be inserted to a depth sufficient to allow the seedling plant to be introduced without crushing or doubling up the roots. The soil should then be firmly pressed down at the roots of the plant with the flat end of the dibber and the thumb and first two fingers of the left hand. Finish off neatly. A good watering in should then be given, and protection from the sun be afforded, if necessary, until established. The plants should remain in these quarters until the Spring of the following year.

If the space at the disposal of the grower is very limited, they may be allowed to flower in these quarters. The practice to be followed in such cases is to note carefully each seedling flower as it opens, and if thought good enough to save and perpetuate, it should immediately be lifted and placed in a specially prepared bed, which has been deeply dug and well manured. In this way, the grower will gradually accumulate several plants of new varieties, if he be lucky enough to raise any worth perpetuating. The growth and other characteristics can then be closely watched, and any plants not coming up to the standard required may be eliminated. The great point to be remembered is never to leave a variety worthy of propagation too long in the seedling bed, among the heterogeneous collection there to be seen, but to lift it as soon as opportunity occurs. If this is not done, the plant is apt to become long and drawn, and most unsuitable for replanting. To this end, therefore, it is wise to give away or destroy any seedling that does not denote some distinct advance on the older varieties, thus giving the remaining seedlings room to develop the more satisfactorily.

On the other hand, if the grower has plenty of space at his disposal, at the beginning of March or earlier, he should plant out the seedlings from which so much is expected into a special bed. Any good garden soil will answer the purpose, but of course it will be an advantage if this has been deeply dug and well manured. The portion of the ground allocated to the seedlings should be well broken up and raked over, and planting be proceeded with forthwith. Select a nice dry day for planting.

The young plants should be lifted with as large a ball of soil adhering to the roots as possible, and a good quantity of soil taken out when planting, so that the roots may be well embedded in their new quarters. A space of about 8 inches should be left between each plant, and the same distance between the rows, and should the weather be dry, a good watering given at the conclusion of their insertion.

Plants with flowers thought to be worthy of reproduction should be marked with a label, and numbered in rotation according to the date of their discovery. Cuttings may be taken from each plant as soon as they are obtainable, and in the following Spring the clumps may be divided up as mentioned hereafter.

A plant should not be heedlessly thrown away without reasonable cause, as the first blooms are not always indicative of the real value of the plant.

Growers possessing a greenhouse, or propagating frame with heat, may equally well sow their seed towards the end of January or beginning of February, and even later. Of course the plants will not flower so early as those sown the previous Summer or Autumn, but they should be in full bloom in mid-July or earlier.

The best method of procedure in this case, is to make use of shallow boxes of about 3 inches in depth, and measuring about 18 inches by 12 inches. Holes should be made in the bottom of these to allow of drainage, and these covered with crocks, which in turn should be covered with any rough siftings that remain over when the ingredients of the compost have been sifted, or with the fibrous part of the loam remaining after sifting.

The box should then be filled with the compost (of the same constituency as that last mentioned) and lightly pressed down.

Having sown the seed in the manner before suggested, a thin covering of the compost should be lightly and evenly strewn over the whole surface, and a gentle watering in afforded by means of a fine-rosed can.

A piece of glass placed over the box will keep the conditions of the soil etc. humid, and thus expedite germination ; but so soon as the seedlings have shown their second leaf, this covering should be taken off to avoid the risk of drawn and weakly plants resulting.

When they have shown their fourth leaf, the seedlings are ready to be pricked off into other boxes, prepared in the same manner. The soil having been made nice and firm, they should be dibbled in about an inch apart, and a gentle watering given. A little sand sprinkled on the top of the soil, previous to pricking off, will greatly assist the plants in establishing themselves. For a dibber use a label with the pointed end slightly blunted.

At this period of their existence, the seedlings are very liable to the attacks of green fly, greatly to the detriment of the plants, which do not appear to be growing at all, and look somewhat sickly. If one of the leaves of a plant be turned up it will be found to be covered with this pest. Steps should be taken immediately to eradicate the evil. A solution of soft soap and water, using 2 ounces of the former to a gallon of the latter, sprayed on with a very fine syringe, will be found to produce the required result.

It is incumbent, therefore, upon the grower, immediately the plants are found to be growing well, to proceed to harden them off, and thus keep clear of this or any other pest brought on by the unnatural conditions under which the plants are raised. The boxes should forthwith be placed in a cold frame, and gradually hardened off.

By about the end of May the plants will be small but stocky plants, and a bed should at once be made ready for their reception. They should be planted in rows about 6 to 8 inches apart, leaving the same distance between the rows. By the middle of July or earlier, the grower should be rewarded by the sight of all the plants blossoming in the greatest profusion.

Note should be made of all the good varieties, and these either removed to a bed by themselves as before mentioned, or marked in some way for taking cuttings or dividing up in the ensuing Autumn or Spring.

As mentioned earlier, the time of seed-sowing is largely a matter of convenience, and providing due prolection be afforded from the elements then existent, seed may be sown at almost any period of the year, and good results accrue.

• Propagation by Cuttings

The primary requisite for the propagation of Pansies by means of cuttings is to possess good, strong, healthy plants from which to obtain them. For this reason, therefore, special care should be taken with plants from which it is intended to propagate, in order that cuttings of the necessary quality and character only may be used, in this way causing greater assurance of success than would otherwise be the case.

If the grower intends to propagate on a very large scale, of necessity special treatment must be accorded the plants in the shape of mulching, manuring, and cutting back the stock plants. Though if only a few cuttings are required, the young basal shoots should be taken, and this may be done without in any way spoiling the flowering effect of the plant ; but as a general rule, growers are always anxious to obtain as many cuttings as possible.

As in the propagation by seed, propagation by cuttings may take place at almost any time during the more genial period of the year. In the case of propagating a particular seedling, or, owing to the fact that stern necessity does not allow the grower to make use of the time generally mapped out for propagation, this becomes a great boon.

Suitable materials in the shape of healthy basal shoots can be used, and providing due protection be given, there is no reason why strong-rooted plants should not result.

However, for the grower who makes a speciality and a hobby of this particular flower, a special time such as, say, the last two weeks in September over which the operation may be spread, will be found the best method. This, of course, is when Spring planting is practised. If the grower requires to plant his Pansies in the Autumn, the cuttings will have to be inserted during June, July and early August, thus allowing plenty of time for good strong plants to be produced for planting out in early October.

Previous to this, the plants should have all the long straggling growths removed, leaving only the young shoots which are breaking away from the base of the plant. To aid the plants in this endeavour—especially in the case of those varieties that are not good bedders—a mulching should be placed around each plant and well worked in with the fingers, the soil round about the base having first been lightly forked over and thereby aerated. The finest mulching material is made up of well decayed manure (spent manure from a mushroom bed is splendid), to which should be added a liberal quantity of coarse road grit. The whole should then be passed through a sieve with about a half-inch mesh. If the plants are not doing well, a quantity of good loam well sifted, and added to the above, will greatly assist to their well-being.

The effect of the mulching will soon be apparent. Acting as an incentive to root action, it will induce the young shoots to throw out roots, and thus cause propagation to be much more easy of accomplishment.

As soon as the plants are in a good condition for taking cuttings, a frame of shallow build, with a moderate slope, should be prepared in which to insert them. If possible a warm but shady aspect should be chosen; and the area within the frame, having been well forked over and levelled, the compost should be introduced.

A series of small frames will be found to answer rather better than one large one, as in the former case the plants can be got at much more easily and attended to with greater comfort. This is worth remembering, as it is well to have all the plants within reach when weeding is necessary, and for any minor attentions which the plants may require. Of course a frame-light will be required over each frame, and this must be kept on during severe weather and until the cuttings are well rooted.

If July propagation is practised, the cutting bed should be in a shady position, and protection given as much as possible from the heat of the sun. A length of thin canvas securely fastened down on the frame-lights maintains the cuttings in fine condition until they are rooted, when the lights should be removed. Air should be admitted during the rooting process by raising the lights as often as possible, and by removing them altogether at night.

The compost used for rooting cuttings should consist of the same ingredients as that advised for seed-sowing, made up as follows: equal parts of loam, leaf soil and sharp sand; to these should be added one part of well rotted horse manure, such as the spent manure from a mushroom bed or cucumber frame. The ingredients should be well sifted, and the whole thoroughly mixed.

When levelled, it should be firmly pressed down with a board or the back of a spade. Great care should be exercised to see that the soil is quite firm, as otherwise

Photo. by J. W. Parkes

VIOLA "LARK." SLIGHTLY EDGED HELIOTROPE BLUE

the cuttings are liable to "hang" and eventually die off. In depth, the compost should measure about 4 to 6 inches, and over its surface should be spread evenly and liberally some sharp silver sand or road grit.

The next question which brings itself before the mind of the grower is the taking and preparation of the cuttings. Cuttings may be divided into two classes: those with little rootlets, and those cuttings that are merely the young shoots which break away from the side and base of the plant. Both are good types of cuttings, but of course the advantage will be with the cutting having the rootlets attached. It was to this end that we advised the use of the mulching material which helps to promote the growth of rootlets on the young basal growths. In such cases half the battle is over, as these will rapidly develop into plants. There is much greater likelihood of their living, and they will quickly pass through that period of apparent standing-still, which cuttings possessing no rootlets pass through during the formation of their first roots. However, it is not always possible to obtain all we want in this way, and in the case of cuttings with no rootlets attached, providing they are inserted in a proper manner, and well looked after, there is no reason why they should not, every one of them, turn out a fine plant in the course of about two months or less.

There is also a third type of cutting which the grower should vigorously eschew. This is known as a stem cutting, and simply consists of one of the more or less hollow stems of a plant. Of course, this is old, and being hollow withal, makes a very bad cutting. Unfortunately, sometimes there are no cuttings to be had from a plant other than these stem cuttings, and in such cases, of course, there is nothing else to do, but to use them; but at the best, they are merely makeshifts, and it behoves the grower to steer clear of cuttings of this description. Such cuttings rarely turn out a success.

The best method of "taking" cuttings is to remove them with a sharp knife, and not to pull them off. Those with rootlets may be plucked off, but care must be exercised not to break them in so doing.

The next question to present itself is that of the preparation of the cuttings. It is obvious that, if all the leaves growing on the basal shoot from which we are to make our cutting are allowed to remain thereon, they would, after insertion in the cutting bed, gradually decay, and cause the cutting to suffer or damp off in consequence. For this reason, therefore, all the lower leaves and bracts should be carefully removed.

The length of the cutting has now to be determined. If it be too long, it will have to be inserted rather deeply into the compost, thus making it more difficult to lift in the ensuing Spring, when a lanky plant in all probability will result. And if too short, it will be impossible, of course, to fix it firmly in the compost. Striking the happy medium, therefore, the cutting when finally prepared should measure about $2\frac{1}{2}$ to 3 inches. It should always be cut through immediately below a joint, with a sharp knife. The accompanying illustrations represent an ideal cutting, and the proper place to cut it through. Of course, if this can be done when taking the cutting from the plant, so much time is saved, but it is not always an easy matter to judge.

In the case of cuttings with rootlets, when removing them from the plant, they should be detached just below the young roots. The bottom leaves, if any, should be trimmed off as above suggested.

If a quantity of cuttings are being taken, it is a good plan to place each cutting, after being trimmed, into a vessel of water. This keeps it fresh and prevents withering.

YOUNG GROWTH DETACHED WITH ROOTLETS
ADHERING. A SURE AND EASY MEANS OF
INCREASING STOCK

AN IDEAL TYPE OF CUTTING, PROPERLY TRIMMED.
THIS SHOULD BE CUT IMMEDIATELY BELOW THE
JOINT, AS MARKED BY THE DOTTED LINE

Some growers, before inserting their cuttings, prefer to dip them in an insecticide to rid them of any aphis or other pest there may possibly be. A good insecticide may be made by dissolving 2 ozs. of soft soap in a gallon of water. A vessel containing this solution may then be placed handy, and the heads of the cuttings dipped therein previous to insertion.

A dibber of much the same kind as that recommended for planting out seedlings—that is, a stick about 8 to 10 inches long and an inch in diameter with a neatly pointed end—should be requisitioned, and a batch of cuttings having been prepared, we may at once proceed to put them in. Care should be taken that a good sprinkling of sand has been spread over the surface, as upon this depends, to a very great extent, the speedy rooting of the cuttings.

A hole should be made with the dibber, bearing in mind the length of the cutting to be inserted. The base of this latter should rest on the bottom of the hole so made. This is absolutely imperative, as will be seen hereafter. The soil should then be pressed firmly downwards against the base of the cutting with the fingers of the left hand and the dibber in the right, so that there may be a proper adhesion of the soil. The compost round about the cutting should then be neatly levelled.

It is apparent that, if, when inserting the cutting, it is not made to rest on the bottom of the hole made for its reception, it will be unable to obtain any nutriment or anything else from the soil, as it will be merely suspended, and failure in rooting will come as a consequence.

A piece of wood, about 3 inches in width and as long as the frame is wide, makes a capital guide, using it both to keep the cuttings in a straight line and to allow a sufficient distance between the rows.

The required number of cuttings having been

inserted, a gentle but thorough watering should be given from a fine-rosed can. This will allow the soil to settle down, but on no occasion should the water be allowed to fall heavily on the cuttings, or disaster may occur in the shape of some of them getting washed up out of the soil.

The frame-light should now be placed on and kept there for a few weeks, and shading afforded when necessary. Air should be admitted, according to the atmospheric conditions prevailing outside at the time, and water given if required. If green fly or red spider make an appearance, a thorough syringing with the soft soap solution, above recommended, will have the effect of clearing the cuttings of these pests. In about a month to six weeks the cuttings inserted in September should be nicely rooted, and before the hard weather sets in should be nice sturdy little plants. When the young plants are well rooted, the frame-lights may be drawn down in favourable weather, thus encouraging the plants to become as hardy as possible for planting out in the ensuing Spring. At any rate this course may be recommended for growers not in the immediate vicinity of large towns, where the smoky and heavy atmosphere which obtains during the winter months proves so destructive—poison-laden as it is—to the young plants. In such cases it would be wise to keep the frame-light on the frames, except on specially fine days.

If the grower intends to practise Autumn planting, the cuttings should be inserted during June, July and early August, in order that the young plants may be sufficiently strong for planting out in October. In this case a shady position should be secured for the propagating bed, and plenty of shade given during the rooting process in the manner before suggested. Air should be admitted as freely as possible. In fact, propagation at this time of the year may be done without the assistance of a frame or frame-light at all, providing the soil in the cutting bed is kept moist, and the cuttings well shaded to prevent undue withering.

During their occupation of the propagating bed or frame, the cuttings should be gone over from time to time, and the soil well firmed either with the fingers or with the edge of a board pressed down between the rows (the former method being the better), to make good any dislodgment which may have occurred owing to worm casts, frosts, etc. If this is not attended to, the cuttings or plants are extremely liable to be lifted out of the soil altogether and ultimately perish. A liberal sprinkling of sand between the rows will help to keep the worms under.

Carefully label each variety as it is dealt with, and, to avoid mistakes, allow a separate row for each kind.

Have a system when propagating; that is to say, have separate frames for, or keep separate in some way, the various types—Pansies, Violas and Violettas. If possible, keep seedling varieties of these in a separate propagating frame; and finally, only propagate the best varieties.

Cuttings may also be rooted in boxes or seed pans. Holes should be made in the bottom of the former, and, these properly crocked, and covered with the rougher siftings of the compost, to allow of drainage. They have no room to develop in these boxes or pans, however, and they should be transferred to the open ground as soon as possible, to allow their roots to develop.

PROPAGATION BY DIVISION OF THE OLD PLANTS

The best time of the year in which to make use of this method of propagation is undoubtedly the Spring. It is at this time that the plants are waking from their

c

Winter's rest; each day brings new life into the old plants, and the leaves and shoots begin to look quite fresh and green.

It is in the Tufted Pansy (Viola) and Violettas that we now see the advantage of the tufted root growth. At the beginning of the year, these old plants should consist of nice circular tufts, from 4 to 8 inches in diameter, each few days showing a marked improvement in their health and size.

The Fancy Pansy, on the other hand, although it may consist of a tuft of a sort (if it be alive at all), is not of the same rooty character as the Viola, but consists, more often than not, of one stem with many lateral growths, which, having but few rootlets, are therefore of less use for breaking up and thus creating new plants. With the majority of Violas, however, almost every little growth in the tuft possesses roots, and is a plant in itself. It will thus be seen what a number of plants can be produced from one tuft. For instance, if one is very short of a particular variety, cuttings may be taken from time to time during the Summer and Autumn, and in the Spring the plant may be broken up to provide further stock. In this way a large number of plants can be obtained. Here again we see the disadvantage of the so-called "Tufted Pansies" that are not tufted, their growth being similar to that of the Fancy Pansy.

A fairly large frame should be placed in a sunny aspect, and the soil therein having been well broken up is prepared in the same way as advocated for propagating cuttings.

Of course, the best plants for the purpose are those forming a nice circular tuft, every individual stem of which is attached to the ground by means of rootlets, or with rootlets breaking away at its junction with the main stem. Each growth will then be a little plant in itself, and only needs to be detached with care, and

OLLOW GROWTH OR STEM CUTTING.   USELESS FOR PROPAGATING PURPOSES

given a short time in the propagating frame to establish itself as a good strong plant.

Plants of this description, however, are not always to be had, and the best must be made of the materials to hand. Always contrive to break up or cut up the old plant, so that as many growths as possible possess roots. If there are any without roots, and stock is limited, by all means place them in the frame. They will root in all probability, though they will be somewhat slower in growing than the others.

The growths so divided should be inserted in the manner suggested when propagating by cuttings, and treated in the same way, though a little more space should be allowed and more air given.

All circumstances being favourable, and with the approach of warmer days (if inserted in the Spring as suggested) nice plants should result in the course of three weeks or a month.

These are then ready for planting out in the beds and borders.

Early blooms may also be obtained from these plants by keeping them in the frames with the lights on. Always be careful, however, that they receive plenty of air, and do not suffer from lack of water.

CHAPTER V

The question as to the correct time for planting is a somewhat vexed one. Some growers advocate Autumn planting, and others Spring planting. Gardeners, it will be found, (especially those who are constantly changing the character of the beds and borders under their management, the beds presenting an entirely different spectacle almost every season) are, as a rule, great advocates of Autumn planting. They like to get the plants in at the end of September or beginning of October, thus getting them well established before the Winter sets in. These will then flower early in the succeeding Spring season, much earlier than if planted in March, and can after a month or two be removed to make room for some other form of bedding plant.

For an early display in the Spring, say at the end of April and early May, it is essential that Autumn planting be practised, as comparatively few of the blooms will be out at that time if the beds be planted during the latter part of March or early April. For later displays, however, Spring planting is quite early enough.

In the case of Spring planting, the grower will not have the trouble of looking after the plants during the trying Winter months, a point worth consideration; and if the plants are not put out until April, which is quite soon enough for Summer and Autumn flowering, they will escape the treacherous east winds, which are so frequently disastrous to plant life.

However, to a great extent, the period for planting

36

bears relation to the object in view. If an early display is desired, then plant in the Autumn. Where an early Summer display is the object in view, Spring planting will be quite early enough.

In the case of some soils, Autumn planting would perhaps be somewhat dangerous. For instance, soils of heavy texture in low and overmoist situations are very poor quarters for wintering plants of the Pansy species in. All Pansies like a soil which contains something they can "hang on" to, and draw upon during the Winter season, but this is impossible of attainment when the conditions are as just described. If the soil at the grower's disposal is of the above described character, then by all means plant early in April.

On the other hand, if the soil is quite satisfactory, and Autumn planting may be practised with less fear of the plants going under, and, providing they get well established before Winter sets in, nice large stocky plants will result in the following Spring.

It will be seen then, that the grower to a great extent is a victim, more or less, to circumstances, and although Autumn planting has great advantages in the shape of sturdier plants and earlier flowers, and should be indulged in wherever possible, Spring planting should be practised if any doubts exist at to the suitability of the ground for planting in the Autumn.

Apart from this question, it would be well for the grower to plant both in the Autumn and in the Spring, in this way securing for himself a constant succession of bloom, whilst at the same time allowing the Autumn planted ones to be cut down to produce stock, in the form of cuttings, etc.

Soil

The first consideration, therefore, if the plants are to be grown in masses for their effect, is to prepare a suitable soil in which they can produce the best results. It is a commonly understood fact that Pansies will grow well in any soil. And so they will, and it is to this fact that we owe so much. But at the same time, if by preparing the soil specially for them, much better results are possible in the shape of larger flowers, healthier growth, and more sustained flowering qualities; it behoves the grower, if he be desirous of letting the plants show their capabilities to the utmost extent, specially to prepare the soil, and so make, at any rate, one factor, and this an important one, conducive to their well-being.

What then is the best soil in which to grow pansies? This, without doubt, is good loamy soil (inclining towards the heavy side if anything), with the addition of horse or cow manure at the time of digging, and in this the plants should do well.

Of course, all soil is not of this description, and the existing soil has to be so modified by means of manure, etc., as to produce the same good result.

If the soil is of *a very sandy character*, plenty of good rotten cow manure should be incorporated. This enables it to retain moisture for a long period, and prevents it from becoming too hot and dry, as otherwise it would be. Pulverised clay and the addition of vegetable manure will also tend to increase its moisture-retaining qualities. Soil of this sandy character is, in its natural state, the worst suited of all for growing Pansies.

Then there is soil of a *light sandy loam* character. Although far better than the last named, this will require the addition of cow manure, though clay may be dispensed with.

As before mentioned, a *good medium loamy soil* is the best suited for Pansy growing, and in this the plants should revel. Soil of this character is sufficiently porous, and at the same time retentive of moisture, keeping the roots of the plant nice and cool in the hot Summer weather. The Pansy is a plant delighting in a cool root run, and in this soil we have all the elements conducive to it.

Finally to treat of *a clay soil.*—This in its natural state is almost, but not quite, as unsuitable for the growing of Pansies as a sandy soil. Being of so heavy a texture, and lacking porosity to a remarkable extent, it becomes impossible for the Pansy roots to penetrate so dense a medium, and plants eventually fail through lack of root action.

However, clay soils can be vastly improved, and are exceeding fertile when once they have been broken up, manure incorporated, and left rough on the surface during the Winter for the frosts to pulverise and sweeten.

The ground should be dug thoroughly, and at the same time every spadeful broken up and pulverised as far as possible. Plenty of sand, together with leaf mould, road grit, ashes, and anything else that will tend to lighten the soil and make it friable, should be added.

Of course, the effect of these modifying elements thus introduced will not show immediate results of a first-class character, and it may take some years even for these operations to bear fruit, and for the ground to become in good working order.

PREPARATION OF SOIL IN BEDS AND BORDERS

Pansies and Violas may of course be planted anywhere, and nothing looks better than bold masses of these flowers in various parts of the garden, and this aspect of their use will be dealt with hereafter more fully. For exhibition purposes, however, a more utilitarian, rather than picturesque, method of growing is necessary when the object is to produce the largest and finest flowers possible. For this reason, it will be found advisable to make use of rectangular beds of a suitable length and width, in order that the various processes and operations necessary for the successful culture of large flowers may take place the more easily.

The most expedient course to follow, therefore, when growing mainly for exhibition, is to prepare beds—according to the number required—of a convenient length, and about 5 feet in width, leaving a space of about 1 foot 6 inches between each bed to form a path. This will allow free access to the beds for all the necessary attentions which must be paid to the plants, if large blooms are wanted by the grower.

The space recommended for the width of the beds will be found convenient in many ways, such as for allowing the plants to be picked over easily, watering, weeding, hoeing, and for many other purposes, thus avoiding trespassing too much on the beds themselves.

But, wherever the plants are to be grown, whether for massing, edging, or in beds for exhibition, to obtain the best results the ground must be thoroughly well dug and prepared.

A trench two spits deep, having first been taken out, the bottom of it should be well forked over. Then should be added a heavy dressing of the manure or other ingredients referred to before, according to the nature of the soil, and upon this should be placed soil to the depth of two spits, a second trench being thus formed which should be treated in the same way until the whole area is covered. In every case the trench should be taken out at least two spits deep, as the Pansy and Viola are deep-rooting subjects, and their roots will soon find the manure, which should make a nice cool root-run for them, and so help them to pass over the trying time in the Summer when the ground above is parched and hot.

If the subsoil, however, is very poor, or the ground is quite new, the method of digging will have to be slightly varied in order that the good soil may be put to the best use possible. The best method by which to treat the soil in cases of this kind is as follows : Starting at one end of the bed remove the good soil as deeply as possible and about 2 feet or so wide, thus making a shallow trench the bottom of which is formed by the subsoil. This should be forked over as deeply as possible, and upon this should be placed the manure, etc., to be incorporated. Then should follow the surface soil taken from the next 1 foot width, thus leaving another trench to be treated in the same manner, and so on, the same method being observed throughout until the whole bed is completed.

If ground with inferior subsoil is treated in accordance with the manner suggested, the best results possible will be obtained, and the plants may confidently be expected to do as well as possible in the circumstances.

However, wherever the Pansies are to be grown, to obtain the best results it will be found expedient to treat the ground wherein they are to be planted by one of the methods suggested above. In short, to grow these flowers well and to obtain the finest results, deep culture is the keynote of success. It is a common error to suppose that Pansies are shallow-rooting subjects; this is not so, and it may come as a surprise to many to learn that frequently, after a season's growth (and this applies more particularly to the tufted section), plants have been found to penetrate over 2 feet in suitable soil in search of moisture and nutriment.

In the first place, assuming that Autumn planting is to be practised, the ground should be prepared as above, during the latter half of August; and, as opportunity offers, it should be gone over with the fork and thoroughly broken up. About the middle of September it should be forked over, and any modifying elements should again be introduced—sand or road grit, ashes, well-rotted cow manure, pulverised clay, etc., according to the character of the soil. The ground having been finally raked over and levelled, the beds may be marked out.

If the plants are to be put in in the Spring, the ground should be well trenched, as above, in the late Autumn if possible, and the weather and frost allowed to get in. Not only will this have the effect of making the soil more friable, but it also will have the effect of killing at least a certain number of insects and weeds. The ground, left in this way, can be broken up with great facility, and late in February it should be forked over and treated in the same manner as suggested for Autumn planting.

Some growers advocate planting early in March or even earlier, in order that the plants may become established in good time, whilst others prefer to wait until the arrival of more genial weather and plant early in April, thus ensuring immunity from severe frosts or the bad effects of the east winds. If a sheltered position can be afforded the plants, and protection given when planted, the sooner they are in their flowering quarters the better. Shelter can generally be arranged for in the shape of an inverted flower pot, and Pansies planted even in April are not averse to this treatment, especially if the position is very exposed or the weather inclement. However, as a general rule, late in March or early in April will be found a very good time for planting; the weather becoming more genial day by day, and the biting effects of the east wind by this time having ceased, the plants should become speedily established.

PLANTING IN THE BEDS

Taking Autumn planting in the first place: the ground should be finally raked over and a "line" placed along each side of the bed, in order to keep the

VIOLA TUFT IN BORDER
By courtesy of Mr W. Sydenham of Tamworth

plants within bounds. Before starting, it is well to make out a list of those to be planted, and so arrange that the colour of each variety harmonises with that of its neighbours, or plant with a view to good contrasts being obtained. For, although the beds are made in a rectangular shape from the point of view of utility, there is no need to bind oneself down by planting in alphabetical order or anything of that sort. Little, if any, good purpose is served in so doing, and although in shape the bed may look somewhat formal and severe, yet this may be taken off to a certain extent if the colours are well blended or contrasted. Dark varieties should not be planted together, but the colour broken up by using a lighter colour between, and so on.

When the plants have been propagated by the grower, they will experience little or no check, and rapidly form fine plants, if lifted and planted in a proper manner. A small trowel should be used to remove the young plants from the propagating frame. A small trowel, such as bricklayers use, answers the purpose splendidly. Being flat and sharp, it can be inserted on either side between the rows, and the plant to be lifted removed without danger of damaging any of the other plants.

For planting purposes a board about 1 foot wide should be requisitioned. This will serve a triple purpose, namely, to keep the rows straight, maintain the rows the same and proper distance apart, and last, but not least, to kneel or stand on when planting, to prevent the soil in the bed being trampled down too much.

Starting at the left hand side of the bed and using the board as a guide, six holes should be made about 10 inches apart. A vessel containing some leaf mould or spent manure, with plenty of road grit incorporated therewith, should be placed handy, and a little placed in each hole. To secure immunity from green fly, etc., each plant, before being inserted, may have its leaves dipped in a vessel containing soapy water (about 2 ounces of soft soap to a gallon of water). The hole, prepared as mentioned, should be of sufficient depth to allow of the plant being inserted just about an inch or so above the point where the off-shoots are beginning to break away.

Holding the plant firmly but gently in the left hand, a handful of the gritty compost should be placed around the roots, and carefully pressed in. Upon this the soil originally removed from the hole should be placed, and this again well pressed down. One row of plants having been put in in this way, the board should be moved back a foot, and the soil round the plants in the completed row be levelled and made neat.

When removing the soil from the next row, start a little way in from the edge of the bed, so that when planted the rows should be after the following pattern :—

.   .   .   .

.   .   .   .   .   .

.   .   .   .   .   .

.   .   .

This will allow the plants as much room as possible.

If the plants are those propagated by the grower himself, they should be lifted with as much soil adhering to their roots as possible. This will necessitate a larger hole to be made for their reception; as it is far better to plant with a large ball of soil adhering to the root of each plant, as it will go ahead much more quickly than if the roots are unnecessarily crushed and the soil removed.

In the case of plants received from the specialist; immediately upon their receipt they should be placed in a suitable vessel and gently sprayed with water from a fine-rosed can. This will have the effect of refreshing them and putting them in a much fitter condition for planting out. It is almost unnecessary to add that they should be placed in a cool and shady position when received. Unfortunately many specialists, when sending out plants, remove almost every particle of soil, leaving only the mass of roots. If plenty of wet moss is used in the packing they will keep fairly fresh, but they are much less satisfactory to plant, and take longer to get into condition and to establish themselves. When ordering plants, therefore, the best plan is to request the specialist to leave as large a ball of soil on as possible. When this is done the plants will arrive quite fresh and quickly become established.

In planting those with little soil attached, the roots should be well spread out and plenty· of the gritty compost used. Care should be taken that they are planted quite firmly.

If the ground be at all dry or the weather hot, plenty of water should be given, but if the soil be damp, it should be withheld until the plants need it.

Protection from the weather should be afforded plants that have been newly set out : from the sun if it is at all strong, and from frosts. An inverted flower pot serves the purpose admirably. It should be removed on all possible occasions, and so soon as the plants have been established, its use should be dispensed with altogether.

In the early Spring, east winds are apt to cause disastrous consequences, and protection from these should be given as much as possible. Pots, pans, baskets, lengths of board, etc., will be found most useful on such occasions.

If the planting has been done in the Autumn, it is well to give the plants a good mulching with *well-rotted* manure. This will help them through the Winter and early Spring, and the grower should be rewarded by good strong plants and a fine display of early flowers.

From time to time, after planting, the hoe should be kept busy between the rows to aërate the soil, and, incidentally, to keep down any weeds which may appear.

Planting in Frames with a View to an Early Display

This is a very useful method of procedure if early blooms are wanted. Planting should take place in the Autumn in shallow frames, the soil in which should be prepared as advised for the outdoor beds. Good strong plants should be lifted and planted about 10 inches apart. A warm aspect should be chosen, and shading and air given if the sun becomes unduly hot; but if the planting is done early in October, this should not cause much inconvenience. Plenty of air should be allowed, and the frame-lights removed altogether whenever possible.

As the severe weather sets in, of course, the frame-lights should once more be brought into requisition, and during the early months of the year the plants soon begin to develop their blossoms. It is in this connection we see the use of the frame-lights. Owing to the state of the weather at this period, the blooms would soon become dirty and damaged if exposed to the open air, so that the frame-lights should now be left on, although at the same time plenty of air should be allowed by propping them open.

The soil in the frame should be constantly looked over, and a mulching of rotten manure given to the plants as they begin to grow. If the plants are treated in this manner, and a sharp lookout be kept for aphides and slugs—which should be dealt with immediately in the manner advocated before—a nice lot of early blooms of large size and good form should result.

An alternative way of securing an early display, is to plant in the Autumn in beds, as before described, and early in March, or still earlier, place frame-lights over the plants therein. A rough framework, and the frame-lights placed thereon, will answer the purpose equally well. This has the effect of bringing the plants along wonderfully, and is a plan that is resorted to by many who want blooms in good time for the purpose of making early displays for the shows.

CULTURE IN POTS

There is yet another way of growing these flowers for exhibition purposes and early displays : that is, their culture in pots. This method of culture applies to the Fancy and the Show Pansies rather than to the Violas or Tufted Pansies and Violettas. It is a practice which has little to commend it, except it be for the purpose of rearing exhibition varieties to produce large and early blooms. It is a practice that cannot be generally recommended, great care having to be exercised in planting and management of the plants so treated, to secure good results.

A compost consisting of one part rotten cow manure, one part loam, one part leaf soil, and one part silver sand or road grit should be made. The ingredients should be sifted with a coarse sieve, and the whole thoroughly well mixed and kept fairly moist and cool till required.

The plants should be placed in 3-inch pots during October. Care should be taken to see that the pots are quite clean, and carefully " crocked " to ensure good drainage ; over the crocks should be placed a little of the fibrous part of the loam, etc., left over after sifting, this preventing the compost from clogging up the crocks, and thus spoiling the drainage—bad drainage being absolutely fatal to success.

Sturdy plants should be taken, and carefully and firmly planted in the pots. A good layer of ashes should be placed in the frame ready for their reception, and on this the pots should stand, thus effectually preventing the ingress of worms. The frame-light should be placed on for protection from severe weather, but air should be admitted on all possible occasions. In this condition the plants should remain until early in February, when they should be repotted into 6-inch pots. The same compost should be used, though in this it need not be sifted, but only the large lumps of loam, etc., be well broken up. Having been repotted, they should be replaced in frames, under the·same conditions, being about 6 inches from the glass, and if treated with doses of liquid manure from time to time, and well looked after in all ways, good large early blooms should be the result. Later on, when the weather is genial, the frame-lights may be taken away altogether, and the plants allowed to grow on of their own free will. Subsequently, after the shows are over, they may be used for propagating purposes. When grown on in this way, however, it is best to plunge the pots in the earth, otherwise the plants may suffer from the heat. Or, as soon as the plants have served their purpose, they may be broken up in the manner suggested heretofore, or, yet again, planted out in the hardy flower garden.

Tufted Pansies and Violettas in Pans and Baskets

This is a capital method of using these types of the Pansy for house or conservatory decoration. Owing to their tufted habit of growth, they are especially suited for this purpose, the other types having much too straggling a habit of growth to justify one in so using them.

Earthenware pans, from 8 inches to a foot or more in diameter, should be procured, with three or four holes in the bottom to allow of drainage.   In depth they should be from 4 to 6 inches.

Having been well crocked, and some of the fibrous part of the loam placed therein for drainage purposes, the pans should be filled level with a compost consisting of equal parts of rotten horse manure, leaf soil, loam, and road grit, all the ingredients being well broken up and mixed together.

A number of plants may be put in, each pan varying according to the size of the plants and the time of the year they are put in.   If planting is to take place in the Autumn, a lesser number will be required than in the Spring, as in the former case they will have more time in which to grow, and thus make larger plants before the flowering period commences.

The plants should be planted firmly, and care should be taken to see that they are arranged equi-distant. They may be treated in the same manner as if they were planted out in the open beds, but the pans should be plunged.

Planting in pans may take place either in the Autumn or Spring, according to the time the blooms are required. If planted in the Autumn, they should be wintered in a cold frame, and the surface soil stirred from time to time, this having the effect of stimulating growth.

It is surprising how well these plants look when in full bloom, and most pleasing effects may be obtained by their use in the house or in the conservatory as subjects for decoration.

All being well, the plants in the pans should last all through the Summer, providing they are plunged in a cool position, gone over from time to time, spent blooms picked off, and straggling growths removed.

The Violettas are especially charming when grown in this way, owing to their less coarse growth and diminutive habit.

D

The pans should be used for indoor decoration in turn, and should not be kept in confined quarters too long, but returned to the garden from time to time to recuperate their lost vigour.

Circular wicker baskets, about 2 feet in diameter, frequently used by nurserymen, also make capital receptacles for plants grown in this way, although owing to the fact of their not being able to be plunged, they require more attention and do not do so well during the very hot weather. These shallow baskets, when placed on the green-sward and the colours well contrasted, create a most pleasing effect.

The above methods may at least be tried, and the grower will be well rewarded for any extra trouble entailed.

Photo. by J. W. Parkes

TUFTED PANSY OR VIOLA "GREY **FRIAR**"

CHAPTER VI

His Pansies having been planted, whether in beds or borders or in whatever position they are placed, and whether grown for exhibition or not, it is naturally the wish of grower to obtain the best results possible. To accomplish this, therefore, it will be necessary to look after the plants in various ways, and their wants, which are but comparatively few, attended to.

Starting in the Spring; as soon as the plants commence to grow, the hoe should be kept busy between the rows in order to aërate the soil. Any blooms that appear should be immediately pinched off, in order that the plant may concentrate its energies in the development of sturdy growth and make a nice healthy specimen. For whatever purpose the plants are being used, much good may be done by giving them a mulching of good rotten manure, with which should be mixed a fair amount of road grit. This should be done about the middle of May and later, the soil having first been well hoed over and any weeds removed. Water should be applied when necessary, and a thorough good watering given, not merely a surface sprinkle, as this serves only to bring the roots to the surface, there to be baked up by the heat.

If the plants for any reason become infested with green fly or red spider a good syringing should be given with a solution of soft soap, all blooms and buds having first been removed and the soil hoed over. Pansies are much more liable to this as well as many other pests than the more hardy Violas and Violettas. At exhibition time, when the plants may happen to be infested with green fly or red spider the only remedy is to use tobacco powder or snuff. This should be dusted on the affected plants. The use of the soft soap solution would mar the blooms irretrievably, and all chance of success would be gone.

Besides aphides, there are some few other unwelcome visitors which cause our pansies to sicken and " go off."

For instance, there is the wireworm, one of the greatest offenders. About an inch long and $\frac{1}{16}$ inch thick this pest has an exceedingly tough skin of an orange-yellow colour. It is more common in new soil, and not infrequently abounds in virgin loam. For this reason a strict watch should be kept for it when dealing with new soil and loam, and an end put to its existence. The wireworm attacks the plant at any point below the ground, gnawing away or puncturing the stem, thus causing it to wither, and eventually die off. There seems to be no other remedy for getting rid of this nuisance, other than being scrupulously careful when digging and sifting, and generally preparing the soil. Dressing the flowering quarters with gas lime in the autumn or digging in a green crop of mustard has materially assisted to rid the soil of this pest. A trap may be made for its capture by inserting a piece of raw potato or carrot in the soil, and this should be inspected from time to time and the delinquents, if any are found within, prevented from doing further mischief by destroying them. Frequently, in the morning a plant may be doing well and look fine and healthy; in the evening it may be a piece of limp green-stuff. Especially is this the case with tap-rooted plants like most Fancy Pansies. As often as not, it is the rarest plant or a particular seedling that is made the subject of this outrage. If noticed in time, the soil may be promptly removed from around the plant and the wireworm caught and destroyed. With the help of a mulching and a good watering, the plant may survive and grow on, but unhappily this cannot always be effected. Of course, the more tufted varieties are much more likely to survive, and in fact very fre quently do, as in this case the plant has its other growths to fall back on, the wireworm seldom attacking all.

Then again, there is the leather jacket grub. This, fortunately, is not so common as the pest before-mentioned, but does quite as much harm. In appearance this creature is of a browny-grey colour, and of an average size of about an inch and a half long and as thick as a lead pencil. The skin is very tough—hence the name—but of a more yielding character than that of the wireworm. It must be destroyed at all costs when caught. Its plan of attack is much the same as that of the wireworm. The only remedy is to keep watch for this depredator when plants are attacked, or when it is suspected of being within the neighbourhood of one's Pansies.

Another depredator which sometimes accounts for plants going wrong and dying off during hot weather, is a millepede of a slatey-brown colour, about half an inch long. This attacks the root of the plant by removing the outer skin of the tender young roots, thus causing the plant to fail. Watering with soot water is advised as a remedy in cases of this kind.

Of course, slugs are almost sure to make an appearance, especially in confined areas, such as small suburban gardens, but soot or lime spread around the plants will quickly act as a deterrent to these abominations.

Plants that have been flowering continuously for some considerable time, and those also in damp situations are not infrequently attacked by a fungoid growth in the form of mildew. To get rid of this, all the blooms should be picked off and the foliage given a good dusting with sulphur. There is another fungoid disease having yellowish brown spots, and is frequently found growing on individual stems of large clumps. Whenever this is seen, the affected stem should immediately be removed and destroyed. Do not throw these deseased pieces on the rubbish heap, but burn them.

To ensure a good long period of flowering, dead blooms should be removed; not cut off, but broken away at their junction with the stem. If dead flowers or parts of the flower stems are left on, they detract from the vigour of the plant and incidentally prevent the development of blooms of good quality.

When plants of Pansies and Violas are being grown for exhibition purposes, still further and more elaborate treatment is needed to bring out the finest qualities in the blooms.

In Pansies and some of the large exhibition Violas, it is necessary to remove all young and weakly shoots at the base, the flowering stems being limited to about five. This should ensure large blooms, as all the vigour of the plant will be transmitted into these stems. In order to give the plants a rest and enable them to obtain increased vigour, all blooms and large buds must be removed some fortnight or three weeks immediately prior to the exhibition. The time allowed will naturally vary according to the state of the weather, but care should be taken always to be on the safe side and allow ample time for the next series of buds to develop sufficiently early for the shows.

In the case of straggling varieties, it will be necessary to peg down the long shoots in order to keep them from being damaged by being blown about by the wind and otherwise spoiled.

From time to time weak doses of liquid manure should be given the plants. Before the manure is used the beds and borders should be hoed over and the plants given a thorough good watering and the liquid manure applied when the soil is quite moist. A good liquid manure may be made by soaking a bushel of either horse, cow, or sheep manure in 30 or 40 gallons of water, and the solution thus obtained well stirred and diluted before use.

For a week or so before the show, the plants will need shading, both as a preventative of the evil effects of dust and rain, and in order to shield the blooms from the burning and withering effects of the sun's rays. There are many means by which this can be done, and large growers generally have some pet system of their own they use.

In cases where the blooms are grown in rectangular beds, a very cheap method of shading may be utilized in the shape of a length of thin canvas or tiffany stretched across the beds. Stout posts should be placed at each end of the beds and a length of stout twine or cord, or better still of wire, should be strained from post to post. If a number of brass rings are now attached to the side of the length of canvas, it can readily be drawn backwards and forwards over the bed along the string or wire.

Another good, though somewhat more expensive, method is to erect a number of posts round the beds and affix on these thin lengths of wood. In this way a support for a number of frame lights can be made. These when covered with paste or lime wash, make an excellent shading medium.

The shading should not be kept on for too long a period, as the plants soon become drawn and spindley, but should be removed on all possible occasions. On clear dry nights this can be done with advantage, and should be done on all other occasions when the weather permits.

When there are a few special plants apart from the others, or in cases where only a few plants are used to pick from, a useful shading may be made by forming a piece of cardboard or paper into a cone, and this fixed in position by means of a stick resting in its apex. A number of these can be made in a very short space of time. If thought necessary and worth while, they may be water-proofed and thus made use of over and over again.

Whatever be the shading medium, care should be taken that it is not too close to the plants, so as to allow not only easy means of access, but also to allow a current of air to be continuously passing over them.

As before pointed out, the shading serves a double purpose, both as regards keeping the blooms from being scorched by the sun, and from being spoiled and damaged by heavy rains.

CHAPTER VII

EXHIBITING

THE best time to pick blooms for exhibiting is in the early morning, as they are then in fine condition, having been refreshed by the cool dews of night.

Blooms should not be cut off, but be broken off at their junction with the stem and leaf. As previously remarked, if any part of the flower stalk is left on, this only detracts from the vigour of the plant. Some varieties break off quite easily, whilst others require a lot of pressure to make them snap off.

Immediately after having been picked, the blooms should be placed in tumblers of water in a cool position. Dust should be carefully guarded against, as this very quickly causes the blossoms to look dowdy.

The two methods in which Pansies and Violas are most commonly exhibited are in sprays of from six to twelve blooms, and in individual flowers set out on a " pansy tray." Both have little to recommend them from a natural and artistic point of view, but as they seem mostly in vogue at the present time a description is here given.

A " pansy tray," which is obtainable of most horticultural sundriesmen, is a rectangular plate of metal in which holes are made, for the insertion of the Pansies, about three inches apart ; under the holes on the underside of the tray run hollow tubes which, when filled with water, keep the Pansy blooms fresh for a considerable time. The foot stalks are shortened and the

Pansy placed in one of the holes of the tray and made to lie as flat as possible. To obtain this flat and often unnatural appearance, the blooms should be taken out of water until they become limp, when the petals can be easily manipulated. It was the custom in days gone by to exhibit Pansies in paper collars, but fortunately, this unsatisfactory and artificial method is giving place to more artistic methods of exhibiting them. A good many growers are now beginning to recognise that to show these flowers in as natural a way as possible, they should be arranged in shallow bowls or vases, and not manipulated by means of tweezers or other implements.

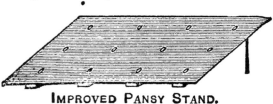

IMPROVED PANSY STAND.

A Pansy Tray for exhibiting purposes. Single blooms are inserted in each hole.

(*Reprinted, by kind permission of Messrs Dobbie of Rothesay, from " Pansies, Violets and Violas."*)

The ancient method may show off the colour of individual blooms to advantage, but for exhibiting a number of blooms, we would rather see a more natural system of arrangement.

Violas are but rarely shown in trays, except it be in order to show off a particular specimen. They are more generally shown in sprays. The making up of sprays is an art which can be learned by practice only. Sprays are made by using rather thin pliable wires, and each piece of wire bent over at one end in the form of a crook. The latter should be placed over the back of the flower where the flower stalk is bent over, by which means it is possible to control the flower quite satisfactorily. Proceed then to bind the wire and flower-stalk together with coarse wool, beginning at the top and winding the wool round the stalk from top to bottom. A piece of foliage should be bound to each flower, and it may be necessary to use fine binding wire to hold this in position. From six to twelve blooms being wired in this way, it only remains to so bind them together, as to form a spray of pyramidal shape. A careful inspection of the sprays exhibited at any of the leading Shows will give a good idea as to the best method of doing this. Broad raffia makes the best medium for binding the flowers together to form the spray, and if a few pieces of moss are worked in at intervals at the same time, it will have the effect of keeping the blooms fresh for some time.

As soon as the spray is finished, it should be placed on its back in a shallow vessel of water, and kept in a cool situation, free from dust, until the time for packing up arrives.

When taking a number of sprays to a distance, the best plan is to cover the bottom of a shallow box with a cloth that has been ·well moistened, and place the sprays face downwards upon this. The whole area at the bottom of the box having been filled in this way, another moistened cloth should be placed over these in turn, and upon this another series of sprays may be arranged and so on. In this way quite a number of sprays may be packed in a small compass, and if speedily attended to on arrival at their destination look none the worse for their journey.

When showing in trays, however, a tin box sufficient to carry about four trays, and especially made for the purpose, should be used. The trays fit in this box on shelves and simply need drawing out and placing on the exhibition table.

For setting up sprays, either boards, in which are inserted tubes containing water wherein to place the sprays, may be used (the boards inclined at a slight angle); or small vases, arranged in tiers, may be utilised with advantage.

Little by little, however, Floral Societies are breaking

away from this stereotyped and inartistic method of showing these beautiful flowers. Instead of making Classes for "sprays" of Pansies or Violas or a number of blooms grotesquely arranged on trays, they not infrequently make use of the term "bunches" instead of "sprays." A fillip is thus given to the man who, unable or unwilling to make a spray, is only too pleased to be able to set up this type of flower in a natural and artistic manner.

These bunches (the number of the flowers to be used generally being specified) may be set up in vases with a wide mouth or in shallow bowls. The flowers should be arranged in the bowls, and foliage worked in separately; but by far the better plan, when exhibiting in this way, is to cut off the whole shoot with flowers and buds. In this form they are not only more easy to arrange, but look better and last longer.

Pansies and Violas exhibited in this way produce a much more pleasing and natural effect, and at the same time create a much greater interest among the general public than when exhibited in the more formal spray.

Another capital way in which to show blooms to their best advantage, when the exhibitor is allowed to put them up in any way he fancies, is to make use of shallow earthenware or metal pans about 8 to 10 inches in diameter and about $2\frac{1}{2}$ inches to 3 inches deep. These should be painted an olive green colour and be filled with silver sand, and the latter thoroughly saturated with water. Foliage should then be cut and placed in the wet sand. The pans are then ready for the flowers, which should be placed in firmly, endeavouring to make the ends of the stalks touch the bottom of the pan. In this way the flowers obtain as much moisture as possible, and, therefore, of course, keep their freshness much longer.

Whatever be the method used, trouble should always be taken to see that the blooms are staged in a way to produce the finest effect. Do not put too many light ones, or have too many dark varieties, together. The colours should be broken up as far as possible, and efforts should be made so to arrange the flowers, that effective contrasts or pleasing harmonies may be created. It adds greatly to the interest of the display if all varieties are named by means of a neat label; in many cases this is a condition of the competition. These remarks apply equally well to Pansies shewn in trays, when the finest blooms should grace the top row, and so on.

It frequently happens that Fancy Pansy blooms are not amenable to the treatment of being made to lie quite flat. This difficulty may be obviated to a certain extent by keeping the blooms out of water for some little time, until they become limp, when they may be subjected to a great deal of pulling about and "dressing" without risk of the petals splitting or becoming damaged. Some exhibitors place a sheet of glass over the blooms, when they have been arranged quite flat, in order to keep them from curling up again after they have been refreshed by a supply of water. The glass, of course, must be taken off as soon as the flowers are staged.

Immediately after staging the blooms, a light sprinkling of water should be given, which will aid them wonderfully in regaining their freshness lost in transit. Before staging sprays, the best plan is to hold them in a vessel of water before placing them in the tubes or vases, allowing the wool and moss to absorb as much moisture as possible. By these means the sprays are maintained in a fresh condition for quite a long time.

CHAPTER VIII

THE USE OF PANSIES AS CUT FLOWERS AND FOR HOUSE DECORATION

PERSONS who have never grown Pansies with a view to their utilisation for house and table decoration, are quite unaware of the beautiful effects obtained by a judicious arrangement of these charming blooms when used as cut flowers. In the case of many of the Violas and all the Violetta type, fragrance alone would seem to demand for them a place in the house.

It is the two latter types which are really the more useful for home decoration, possessing as they do a lightness and brightness not obtainable with the Fancy Pansy.

Pleasing and charming decorations may be made in shallow bowls, with a happy blending of colours ; and for a pretty effect on the table, a few small vases, each filled with a given variety of one of these flowers, cannot be surpassed.

With the help of the endless variety of stands and floral aids now on the market, delightful table decorations may be made with Pansies and Violas. Their own foliage may be used, and this, with the aid of few pieces of hawthorn, horn-beam, or similar spriggy growths, produce a most charming effect.

The harmonious blending of the colours should be borne in mind, and, if the decorations are required for use under artificial light, note should be made of those which look best in such circumstances. Rich self

Photo. by J. W. Parkes

VIOLA PRIMROSE DAME. BLOOMS ARRANGED IN A SAUCER FOR TABLE DECORATION, ETC.

colours, such as dark yellow and purple, show themselves to great advantage by artificial light, and grand
contrasts may be obtained in this way.

A most interesting and pleasing method of decorating
with Pansies is to make use of the shallow pans or
saucers referred to in methods of exhibiting. These
should be painted green, both to keep the water from
percolating through the porous substance (if they are
earthenware), and also for artistic reasons. These should
be filled with sand, as suggested, which should be
thoroughly saturated with water. Foliage should be
liberally made use of, and the blooms arranged as
naturally and artistically as possible. Saucers used in
this way may be placed anywhere, and will be sure to
render a good account of themselves owing to their
refreshing and novel appearance. Much can be done
also with seed-pans and baskets with growing plants
therein, as before mentioned. These, as before remarked, should not be kept indoors too long, however,
but should be returned to the open in order to keep
them in good health.

As button-hole flowers, Pansies are very striking,
whether used in the shape of a spray or in a small bunch ;
Violetta Pansies look especially sweet when worn as
button-hole flowers. The only drawback to their use
in this way is that they comparatively soon begin to
fade, unless kept in a tube with water in it.

CHAPTER IX

PANSIES IN THE FLOWER GARDEN AND HARDY BORDER

There are few hardy flowers that give such a wealth of display and continuity of flowering as the Pansy. Commencing to flower early in the Spring and continuing far into the Autumn, it is obvious that their sphere of usefulness is much greater than that of the average hardy plant. Specially delightful are these flowers when used as edgings. Not necessarily formal straight edgings, but planted so that the line becomes a wavy mass of colour. It is in cases such as this that the Tufted Pansies, or Violas, and Violettas are again seen to so much greater advantage than the Fancy and the Show Pansies. Not only is this due to their free flowering qualities being so much better, and the far longer period they are in flower, but owing to the fact that they are far more useful for colour effects. Being obtainable in almost every shade of colour, most delightful floral pictures may be created by an artistic blending of colours, or striking contrasts created by planting different varieties in masses in close proximity one with another. Beds made on a gentle slope, planted wholly with Violas, look superb if a judicious colour blending or contrast be effected. In Regent's Park there is an undulating bed which for many years past has been planted with Violas almost exclusively, and very pretty it has always looked.

Then, apart from being useful for edgings and massing, the delicate shades of the Tufted Pansy make an ideal groundwork for taller growing plants, such as Carnations, Fuchsias, Wall-flowers, and many other hardy plants. Long after these latter have ceased blooming, and have been cut down or removed, the Violas will still be growing and covering the ground with their bright colours.

Violas planted as a groundwork to Roses are simply superb, and little by little the garden-loving public are beginning to realise that beautiful harmonies may be made by planting Violas of some of the beautiful soft colours now obtainable around their Rose bushes, thus not only ensuring a bright display when all else is blank and uninteresting, but forming a delightful spectacle when the Roses are in full bloom.

There are many gardens which, at certain seasons of the year, are to some extent blank and colourless, owing to the plants therein either having flowered, or not yet come into flower. By a suitable planting of Violas, the uninteresting time may be bridged over admirably, and the erstwhile wilderness turned into a place of brightness, long before the Roses are in bloom.

Then again, Violas planted in fairly large masses, make an excellent foreground for all sorts of taller growing herbaceous plants. Some of the " Fancy " type of Violas planted in this way give splendid results. Or, a groundwork of an orange-yellow Viola, say, " Miss E. M. Cann," with a background of dark blue Delphiniums, together create a splendid effect.

It will be seen, therefore, that with a little thought and by experiment, most delicious effects may be obtained by means of the flowers of the Tufted Pansy, no matter whether used by themselves or in conjunction with other hardy plants.

A point worth remembering in this connection is that these flowers, which always turn towards the light, lose much of their brightness and richness, and therefore to

E

a certain extent their effect, when planted in a position in which their faces cannot be seen. Care, therefore, should be taken when planning the situation of the bed, to ascertain the effect of the sun upon it, and note the best point of vantage from which the brightest effect is obtainable.

Pansies and Violas may be planted in the same situation year in and year out, provided the soil in the bed is renewed frequently—every year if possible. Otherwise, they will not remain in nearly such a healthy condition and give such good results, and possibly will begin to fail just as the plants should be at their best.

CHAPTER X

VIOLETTAS OR MINIATURE TUFTED PANSIES

WITH the advent of a seedling raised by the late Dr Charles Stuart, a new type of the Pansy has sprung into existence. Unlike most raisers, Dr Stuart worked on definite lines, and his seedlings were either the results of direct crossings with *Viola cornuta* or with other seedlings having *cornuta* "blood" in them. From this it may be assumed that "Violetta" is a descendant of *Viola cornuta*, and as such possesses the characteristics of hardiness and tufted habit common to Alpine plants. Curiously enough Dr Stuart was not looking for any particular form of flower, but was keeping a sharp look-out for a Viola which did not possess rays. In "Violetta" he found his great improvement, and at the same time brought into prominence another new type. He was at once attracted by the delicious perfume, and immediately had the plant pulled to pieces and propagated, thus creating a good stock for the ensuing year. This took place in 1887, and from that time forth, he was always at work raising new varieties.

The raising of a plant with its flowers possessing no rays was a great advance, and many years might have elapsed before another chance such as this revealed itself, for it is more than probable that the majority of Violas in existence to-day which are rayless, owe it to the fact that they are associated in some way, however remote, with "Violetta" and other varieties the result of crosses with *Viola cornuta*.

Dr. Stuart and some few other raisers continued to work on these lines, and many beautiful things were produced. In the majority of cases the resulting seedlings were larger that Violetta, but had the same style of growth and other characteristics similar. In general, their growth may be described as procumbent and tufted to a degree, the stems being very short jointed, and numbers of shoots are emitted through the soil from the base ; if left in the same position for two or three years they are one mass of roots and practically perennial. The flowers are borne on stiff erect footstalks, and as a rule, well above the foliage.

The similarity of these somewhat larger flowers of the Violetta type led to confusion in their classification, as they seemed to be too large to call Violettas, and not large enough to be classed with the larger flowering kinds. However, the size has gradually increased in the newer varieties, and this question should no longer arise. To demonstrate the confusion which existed in the early days of the Violetta, a short extract from a lecture given by Mr W. Baxter at the Viola Conference in 1896 may be given. Speaking of exhibiting miniature Violas, he drew attention to some of the smaller Violas being included as Violettas, and therefore disqualified in a recent show. He went on to say, " No attempt was made to grow them large, in fact the effort was in the opposite direction. This leads up to the principal point for which I wish to contend, viz.: a miniature should be a miniature, without allowing room for a premium on bad cultivation."

At the Viola Conference in 1894 certain rules to define the properties of Violettas were adopted. These are :—

First: Form.—The flowers may not be circular as in the florist's Pansy, but may be narrow and more oval in form, and the petals smooth and of good substance.

A SMALL BOWL OF VIOLETTAS, "QUEEN OF THE YEAR"

Second: Colour.—The colour should be bright, clear and striking, whatever the shade. The eye should be bright gold or orange, and may run into the lip on the under petal, but no *central ray or marking is admissible,* and whether shaded, edged, or self coloured, the colours should be well contrasted.

Third: Fragrance.—The flowers should be highly perfumed, which property is one of the invaluable charms of the type.

Fourth: Size.—Size, as a point of excellence in this type, deserves consideration, as we depart from the broad lines generally laid down for florist's flowers, and consider the flowers should not be more than $1\frac{1}{2}$ inches across as a maximum and 1 inch across as a minimum. Flowers ranging between these sizes will afford ample ground for admiration, and will be more suitable for small glasses, or the exhibition spray.

Fifth: Habit.—The habit of the plants should be dwarf and procumbent, the foliage small and bright, the leaves close together, the joints short, and the habit bushy, with stalks of such length as will bring all the flowers well together.

The above may be taken to set out correctly the salient features of the miniature type, although as to the flowers not being circular in shape, and less than 1 inch wide, these are mainly matters of taste, as there are some very beautiful little things not conforming with these ultra strict rules.

The growing of Violettas, however, did not " catch on," and until quite recently the type had almost been dropped altogether. This lack of interest and attention had evidently been due to the want of a proper understanding of the growth and use of these delightful plants. Too much was expected of them. Specialists and others who started to grow these miniature sorts forgot that whilst they were small in flower, they were also small in growth.   They therefore expected them to be as coarse and strong growing as the larger types, and were disappointed when it was found that the plants did not make so much growth as was anticipated. To realise their full value and worth in the garden, the plants should be left in their flowering quarters for two or three years in succession without being in any way disturbed at the roots.   At the end of this time, they will be delightful tufts, 18 inches or so across, and blossoming in the greatest profusion during their recognised period of flowering.

During the last year or so, however, a little more interest has been shown in Violettas, and persons possessing rock gardens are beginning to realise their immense usefulness in this direction.   This, in all probability, is due in no small measure to the more recent additions to the lists of the miniature varieties, which eclipse most of the older varieties in every way. These newer varieties are stronger growing, very free-flowering, longer-stemmed and produce their flowers, as a general rule, earlier in the season than most of the original varieties.   The substance of the flowers, too, in many instances shows distinct improvement.

In addition to the dozen or so Violettas in commerce a few years ago, we have produced some forty new varieties, all quite distinct, and of colours hitherto unknown in this type.   The colours now range from white, blush, orange, yellow, blue in varying shades, to even edged varieties.   These, as is apparent, are a distinct advance, and in time there is no reason to doubt but that the colours will be as varied in the Violettas as in the larger flowered Tufted Pansies.

Especially suited are these charming little flowers for the rock garden.   Here they can remain and thrive undis turbed, giving evidence of their extreme usefulness for this branch of their culture by continuous flowering and delightful fragrance. Being true Alpines in habit and character, they are ideal plants for this purpose. At the time the Violettas are coming into flower, the rock garden, as a rule, is beginning to look less interesting, and as the season advances this fact becomes more apparent. How delightful it would be, therefore, in order to avoid the unkempt look of the rock garden at this period, if Violettas were planted in suitable positions, and thus materially add to its charms and brightness. The ordinary Tufted Pansies or Violas would in most instances be too coarse in growth to produce such a good effect, but the miniature-flowered varieties are specially adapted for use in this way, owing to their distinctly neat and tufted appearance. Alpines as they are, and deep rooting subjects withal, their roots will find their way deep in the cooler soil beneath, in this way enabling the plant to withstand, without dire effects, the full effects of the sun's rays.

Dead and damaged blooms should be picked off as often as opportunity occurs, in order to keep the plants in good health as long as possible.

Then again, Violettas may be used for planting in walls, between flagstones, along edges of walks, and a hundred and one other ways, and will amply repay the grower with their daintiness. Their fragrance alone, quite distinct from that possessed by any variety of Tufted Pansy, is quite sufficient inducement to create a demand for these gems, when more widely known and recognised ; and we cannot do otherwise than believe, that, as time goes on, this type of the flower will be as extensively cultivated, and be as popular as the larger flowered varieties are at the present time.

A list of the more noteworthy varieties of those recently raised by my father, Mr D. B. Crane, and of other really good sorts, is given elsewhere.

CHAPTER XI

RAISING NEW VARIETIES FROM SEED AND METHOD OF CROSSING

THANKS to the facility with which the various types of the Pansy are fertilised by numerous insects, the raising of new varieties is rendered comparatively easy of accomplishment, and aided by various processes of selection many very fine varieties have been introduced.

Success in raising new and striking flowers is due in a great measure to the fact of having a large and comprehensive collection of plants from which to select. This is when hybridisation is left to the agency of insects, though of course where artificial hybridisation is resorted to, the collection of flowers need not necessarily be at all great.

If the centre of a Pansy bloom be carefully inspected and pulled to pieces, it will be seen to consist of a conical-shaped ovary, at the apex of which is produced the pistil which terminates in a round stigma, the under portion, which overhangs the yellow "eye" of the flower, being hollow and secreting a viscid matter. The anthers surround the ovary and pistil, and secrete the pollen grains before they are scattered in the channel formed by the junction of the bottom petal with the spur, and upon the hairs within which the grains are suspended. In this latter position, by means of visiting insects, they will soon either become transferred to the stigma of their own particular flower, or some of the grains will be transferred to the stigma of another flower or flowers. The method by which insects accomplish this is clearly shown in the extract from Professor Hillhouse's Paper at the Viola Conference in 1895 given heretofore (pp. 5 and 6).

Assuming fertilisation, therefore, is left to chance, it will be seen that the resulting seedlings will naturally be of considerable variety, that is, if the collection of plants embraces a good number of varieties. In this way good new varieties are frequently raised. However, year by year, it becomes increasingly difficult to obtain something quite distinct and striking and also first-class, owing to the large number of really good varieties already in cultivation.

For this reason, therefore, and in order to be more certain of obtaining new " breaks," resource must be had to artificial fertilisation of the flowers. By this means, it is possible in a small way to control the colour and certain other characteristics in the resulting seedlings. Cross fertilising, therefore, should not be done in a haphazard manner, but what the result of the fusion of two dissimilar varieties will probably be should be borne in mind and striven after.

Then again, as a good habit in these plants should always be steadfastly sought after, the seed-bearing plants should possess a good habit.

An easy way of cross-fertilising is as follows :—The flower from which the pollen is to be obtained having been selected, the lower petal should be removed, care being taken not to scatter the pollen in so doing. A small camel-hair brush should then be taken and passed gently along the hairy channel, which contains the pollen, collecting as much as possible on the point of the brush. This should then be inserted with the greatest care into the hollow stigma of the flower which is to be the seed-bearer, the viscid matter in which will collect the pollen from the brush. The flower should then be marked in a suitable manner to distinguish it from others.

Another way is to slightly and carefully pull down the bottom petal of the seed-bearing flower, and to insert along the inside of its channel-like formation the lower petal from the pollen-bearing flower, so that the stigma rests upon the petal so inserted, holding it in position. In this way some pollen grains will be introduced into the stigma, and fertilisation take place.

Careful growers place a small muslin bag over flowers fertilised in this way, in order to prevent the ingress of insects, which might possibly spoil the hybridiser's plans.

A bright day should, if possible, be chosen for the operation of cross-fertilisation, and care should be taken to see that the flowers used are quite fresh, and have also reached maturity.

Seed pods should be left upon the plant until they are as ripe as possible; that is to say, just prior to bursting point; a safe time to pick them off being when the pod stands straight out in line with the flower stem. The best plan is to pick the whole stem and not merely the pod. These should be placed in muslin bags and hung up in a warm or dry situation. In a week or so some of the pods will have burst, and when this has taken place throughout the whole series of pods, the seeds should be sifted and placed in a tin, and kept in dry quarters until required for sowing.

There are several of the viola species which have not been used for cross-fertilisation purposes, and who knows if a number of experiments be made in this direction, whether yet another type of the Pansy awaits us? There is plenty of scope for work in this direction.

As to Sports

There are many Violas, and Pansies too, which during the flowering season lose their colour, or " sport," and are frequently quite out of character, especially in hot weather, and during periods of drought.

VIOLA HARRY BAMBER"

Not infrequently, a plant persists in sporting, and this sport can be perpetuated by means of cuttings. Quite a number of some of those now grown came originally by way of sports; as for instance, *Viola* " White Duchess," from " Goldfinch "; and *Viola* " J. B. Riding," from " William Neil."

CHAPTER XII

THE BEST TWENTY SHOW PANSIES

White Grounds:—
Agnes Kay.
Miss Silver.
Mrs Brown.
Mrs M. Stewart.

Yellow Grounds :—
Busby Beauty.
James Craik.
James Harvey.
John Kirkwood.

White Selfs :—
Annie Muir.
Bobby Harper.
Busby White.
Purity.

Yellow Selfs :—
Annie D. Lister.
Busby Yellow.
John Henderson.
Mrs W. P. Crosbie.

Dark Selfs :—
A. Lewis.
Dr Inch.
Leslie Melville.
Wm. Fulton.

THE BEST TWENTY-FOUR FANCY PANSIES

Annie D. Lister.—This flower possesses a splendid large blotch, margined with creamy white; the top petals are of a light violet in colour, with a broad margin of creamy white. This is a beautiful light coloured variety, and grand size and form.

Blue Gown.—A new variety of a fine bright blue colour,

of good shape and quality, and keeps its colour well throughout the season.

Colin Pye.—A well known sort, possessing a large violet blotch, edged rosy-purple. The upper petals are white, with a band of rosy-purple. One of the most constant and reliable Pansies in cultivation, every bloom coming large and true.

Col. M. R. G. Buchanan.—One of the finest varieties in existence. The blotch is of dense rich dark brown colour, broadly margined amber-yellow, top petals violet and amber. A flower of large size and splendid substance.

C. K. Pooler.—An immense blotch of a mulberry tint, laced with pale yellow, upper petals deep heliotrope. This variety possesses in a marked degree the ideal shaped bottom petal, which extends completely across the wing petals.

David Wilson.—A large, well-shaped flower, with a large violet blotch, margined crimson and white, and upper petals the same colour as the margins.

Dr M'Diarmid.—One of the best varieties ever raised, with large black blotch of circular shape, belt yellow, and upper petals same colour, blotched and rayed with black.

Effie R. Wilson.—Another very fine flower of large size, with immense violet blotch, belted white, and upper petals same colour as blotch.

George Stewart.—Fine large flower, with a chocolate coloured blotch, edged golden yellow. Upper petals yellow, flaked with crimson.

Henry Stirling.—A flower of striking colour and immense size, brownish-black blotch, margined yellow, suffused with crimson, top petals yellow belted with crimson.

Jeanie R. Kerr.—A very good quality flower, with brown-violet blotch. Upper petals yellow, edged white.

Jessie L. Arbuckle.—One of the most constant flowers raised, large circular blotch of blue colour, margined white, top petals purple and white.

Lord Roberts.—A very large and perfect flower. A prune-coloured blotch, laced yellow and carmine, top petals yellow and carmine.

Maggie Watson.—This is a very large flower, possessing an immense deep plum-coloured blotch, edged white. Upper petals are white, in Spring and Autumn heavily pencilled with heliotrope.

Miss Neil.—This variety possesses a flower of very great substance, with a large velvety blotch, edged white, laced with crimson. Upper petals white, pencilled with crimson and purple.

Mr B. Welbourne.—A handsome and striking flower, with a clear-cut brownish-black blotch, edged with primrose. Upper petals a bluish-drab shade.

Mrs John Lister.—A most distinct and beautiful variety, with large dark violet blotches, broadly margined with cream. The top petals are purple, shaded mauve and cream.

Mrs Maundril. — A very fine quality flower. Beautiful dense circular blotches, with a margin of white, upper petals purple and white.

R. C. Dickson.—A large and very fine flower, with dark crimson blotch, edged rose. Top petals cream spotted with rose.

Sam Craig. — A splendid variety for competition. Bright yellow self of great size and substance, with rich glossy circular black blotch. Perfectly formed under petal.

Susan Stuart. — A grand flower with dark blotch, margined with yellow, top petals yellow, heavily marbled heliotrope.

W. B. Child.—One of the best varieties in cultivation, possessing a large glossy purple blotch, edged yellow and gold, upper petals deep yellow and purple.

Twenty-four Violas or Tufted Pansies for Exhibition

(Preference being given to those varieties which possess a fair habit.)

Admiral of the Blues.—A fine deep blue self, with yellow eye, rayless; a bloom of very fine quality. Habit, fairly good.

Cream King.—A large circular cream self, rayless, fair habit; very fine in early Summer.

C. Y. Coates.—An enormous flower of splendid substance; light yellow, faintly rayed early in the season. Robust constitution and free flowering. Good bedder.

Effie.—A white ground, with very broad belt of violet; upper petals rosy-purple. A strikingly beautiful flower.

General Baden-Powell.—Large orange self, rayless. A very large flower, but rather poor habit.

Goal-Keeper.—Fine rich purple self, slightly rayed. Good bedder.

Hawke.—White, edged deep bluish-purple. Rayless in warm weather. Fair habit.

Helen Smellie.—White ground, distinctly edged with light bluish-purple. Good bedder. A very fine variety.

J. H. Watson.—A grand flower of reddish-purple, streaked with magenta and white. Good bedder. One of the finest Violas raised.

John Wyllie.—A fine large flower; colour, rich crimson-purple, the top petals lighter. A bloom of very fine quality, and the plant possesses a good habit.

Lady Grant.—Large white ground slightly rayed, edged deep bluish-purple. Good habit.

Lizzie Storer.—Glossy black under-petal, tipped with lavender. Other petals lavender. Poor habit.

Maggie Currie.—An immense flower of great substance. Colour soft rose, striped dense purple.

May.—A very large and handsome rich orange-yellow rayless self, of good form, and splendid substance. Good habit, and free flowering.

Mary Burnie.—A ground of creamy-white, rayless, and edged dark heliotrope; an extremely large and fine flower.

Minnie J. Ollar.—A large flower. Colour, creamy centre and heavily edged plum-purple. Poor habit. Free flowering.

Miss Anna Callan.—Pale lavender, deepening towards the edges.

Mrs Chichester.—Marbled purple on white ground, very large; useful for all purposes. Good habit and strong grower. Extremely free flowering. Very consistent.

Mrs T. W. R. Johnstone.—Upper petals mauve, under petals glossy black blotched mauve. Fair habit.

Peace.—Chaste creamy-white rayless flower, tinted pale heliotrope. A very beautiful variety. Splendid quality.

Sunbeam.—Primrose yellow, picoteed blush heliotrope, large circular rayless flower. Good habit.

White Empress.—Large creamy-white flower. Rayless. Good bedder. Free flowering, and strong constitution.

Wm. Lockwood.—Immense rayless yellow bloom of very good quality. Indifferent habit. Coarse grower.

Woodcock.—Large oval-shaped flower, white, with pale lilac border. Slightly rayed, but very refined. Good bedder.

TWENTY-FOUR TUFTED PANSIES BEST SUITED FOR BEDDING PURPOSES AND MASSING

Acme.—A very useful sort for massing, though the flower is not of the best quality. Colour, bright purplish-crimson, with bright eye. Strikingly effective.

A PLANT OF A TUFTED PANSY IN FULL BLOOM, AFTER A SEASON'S GROWTH

By courtesy of Mr. W. Sydenham of Ta worth

Bessie.—Rayless blush self, very delicate tint, strong grower and profuse bloomer.   Extremely free flowering.

Blue Gown.—A beautiful free-flowering plant, with a dwarf habit.   Colour mauve-blue, rayless.   Ideal.

Bullion.—Rich golden-yellow flower, rayed, extremely free flowering.   Very compact and dwarf habit, but poor quality flower.   Popular for both early and late displays.

Bridal Morn.—Very effective shade of pale heliotrope-blue, rayless.   Fair habit.

Cottage Maid.—A very effective bedding sort of the fancy type.   Colour purple and lavender, blotched white.   Most consistent.

Councillor Waters.—Crimson-purple, a dark self colour; profuse bloomer.   Dwarf habit.

Daisy J. Wright.—A pretty plum-coloured fancy flower, after the style of "Cottage Maid."   Quite a new shade in this type of flower.   Free flowering and very effective.

Duncan.—A striking deep bluish-purple self, very slightly rayed.   Good habit, free flowering.

Duchess of Fife.—A well known edged variety. Colour—primrose, distinctly margined blue; a splendid dwarf, creeping-like habit.   Free flowering.

Ethereal.—Very beautiful flower of a delicate heliotrope hue, rayless, and sweet-scented.   Delightfully close tufted habit.   Quite distinct.

Florizel.—Pale blush-lilac rayless flower.   Sweet-scented, and splendid dwarf habit.   Beautiful plant when once established.

Goldfinch.—Another flower similar to "Duchess of Fife," but colour is deeper, being yellow.   One of the best varieties for bedding, having a beautiful dwarf, creeping-like habit.

J. B. Riding.—Bright purple, slightly rayed, very useful for massing.   Striking colour.

John Quarton.—A very free-flowering sort; colour, light mauve-blue self.   Very slightly rayed.

Marian Waters.—Pale rosy-lilac bloom, slightly rayed, sweet-scented, and strong grower. Beautiful late in the year.

Mary M'Lean.—Large, light blue rayless self, with neat yellow eye ; a good colour, and very free flowering. Capital bedding habit.

Miss E. M. Cann.—A rich orange-yellow flower of oval form, rayless in warm weather. Free flowering in the extreme, and most effective for massing. The best of its kind. Sweet-scented.

Mrs E. A. Cade.—One of the best bedding kinds in cultivation, bright rayless yellow, with orange-yellow centre. Sweet-scented. Perpetual bloomer.

Primrose Dame.—Primrose self with orange eye, and slightly rayed in the early summer. A most persistent bloomer, and fine for massing. Strong grower.

Rolph.—Another very useful sort for massing ; grey-blue self, rayed.

Rosea Pallida.—Same type as " Blue Gown "; pale blush-lilac in colour, and rayless. Creeping-like style of growth.

Swan.—Pure white, with large square orange eye, rayless, very effective. Beautiful habit and free flowering.

Woodcock.—Very dwarf habit, large white flower of oval shape, with pale lilac border. Charming habit.

TWENTY-FOUR OF THE BEST ALL-ROUND VARIETIES OF TUFTED PANSIES OF GOOD QUALITY. ONLY THOSE WITH A GOOD HABIT ARE INCLUDED

Admiral of the Blues.	*C. Y. Coates.*
Bessie.	*Duchess of Fife.*
Bridal Morn.	*Duncan.*
Cottage Maid.	*Ethereal.*
Cream King.	*Florizel.*

Goldfinch.
J. H. Watson.
John Quarton.
Lady Grant.
Marian Waters.
Mary M'Lean.
Miss E. M. Cann.

Mrs Chichester.
Mrs E. A. Cade.
Peace.
Primrose Dame.
Swan.
White Empress.
Woodcock.

Eighteen best rayless Tufted Pansies. Only those of Good Habit are included

Admiral of the Blues.
Bessie
Bridal Morn.
Blue Gown.
Cream King.
Ethereal.
Florizel.
Helen Smellie.
Miss E. M. Cann.
Mrs E. A. Cade.
Peace.
Royal Purple.—Very effective free-flowering bedding sort; colour—royal purple, with neat yellow eye.

Seagull.—Pure white, neat yellow eye; splendid bedder.

Mary Hope.—Pure dead white, very tufted.

Swan.
Rosea Pallida.
Woodcock.
White Empress.

The Best Eighteen Violettas

Blanche.—Clear silvery white, quite distinct; not buite as free flowering as some of the newer kinds, however.

Commodore Nutt.—Bright yellow circular flower, very charming. Compact habit.

Cynthia.—Pale blush-lilac of oval form, yellow eye; delightful creeping habit, and very long footstalks. New.

Diana.—A beautiful primrose-yellow flower suffused yellow, oval in shape; quite a distinct advance. Fine long footstalks. New.

Eileen.—Charming deep blue flower, neat yellow eye;

extremely free flowering, and very strong constitution. Persistent bloomer. New.

Estelle.—One of the smallest of the miniature section. Pure white, slightly suffused yellow on the lower petals. New.

Forget-me-Not.—One of the older Violettas. Rather larger flower than the original " Violetta " and the newer kinds. Colour—bluish-lilac with white centre ; very free.

Lavinia.—Beautiful blush-lavender, veined a deeper shade, splendid creeping habit. A lovely acquisition. New.

Gertrude Jekyll.—A most dainty little circular-shaped flower ; a perfect bi-colour, lower petals rich yellow, upper petals primrose. Very distinct. New.

Olivia.—A most dainty flower, colour—white, faintly tinted lavender-blue ; yellow suffusion on lower petals. Long footstalks. New.

Purity.—An improved form of the original " Violetta," fine substance in the petals. Colour—pure white, heavily suffused with yellow on lower petals. Long footstalks. New.

Queen of the Year.—China blue in colour, sometimes flecked with white. Circular shape. Quite distinct. Scarce.

Rock Blue.—Charming little deep blue flower, effective yellow eye ; a perfect gem. New and choice.

Robbie Jenkins.—A most delightful little flower of perfect form. Another minute-flowered variety ; white, very deeply suffused yellow on lower petal. New.

Sweetness.—One of the most minute blooms of this type ; white, with yellow eye. Long footstalks. New.

Thisbe.—Beautiful pale blush flower, with yellow eye ; beautiful compact habit. Long footstalks. Dense tuft. New.

Violetta.—The original of the type, pure white, suffused yellow on lower petals. Long footstalks.

Winifred Phillips.—Very pretty little flower, edged and tinted blue on white ground; quite distinct. New.

The foregoing are the crème de la crème of all the Violettas in existence, and include shades of colour and quality of flower hitherto unknown in this type. Of the older varieties, only six are deemed worthy of insertion; those omitted being of very indifferent quality, both in bloom and growth, and evidently merely poor specimens of the larger Tufted Pansy and not true Violettas. These latter also possess little or no scent. Every variety in the above list is beautifully sweet-scented and has an ideal habit of growth.

CHAPTER XIII

THE VIOLET

THE modest Violet is a most welcome flower, whether growing wild in the hedgerow or bank, or cultivated and made much of in our gardens. Blooming, as it does, at a time when most other subjects are past, or not yet showing flower, it is all the more appreciated, and doubly so when it " droops its soft and bashful brow, and from its heart sweet incense fills the air." For, undoubtedly, much of the esteem in which these modest flowers are held is due to their delicious scent.

The violet in its various forms holds quite a place in poetry, due, in no small measure, to the modesty with which this flower is indelibly associated, owing no doubt to the lowly habit of growth and the retiring appearance of the plant with its drooping flowers. The poet Barton draws a most delightful word-picture of this characteristic in these modest little flowers.

> " Beautiful are you in your lowliness,
> Bright in your hues, delicious in your scent ;
> Lovely your modest blossoms, downward bent,
> As shrinking from your gaze, yet prompt to bless
> The passer-by with fragrance, and express
> How gracefully, thought mutely eloquent,
> Are unobstrusive worth and meek content
> Rejoicing in their own obscure recess.

Bowring sees them in much the same light :—

> " Sweet flower ! Springs earliest loveliest gem l
> While other flowers are idly sleeping,
> Thou rearest thy purple diadem ;
> Meekly from thy seclusion peeping.

Thou, from thy little secret mound,
Where diamond dew-drops shine above thee,
Scatterest thy modest fragrance round ;
And well may Nature's Poet love thee ! "

The delight with which its advent is hailed, is expressed with great depth of feeling in the following lines :—

"Sweet lowly plant ! once more I bend
To hail thy presence here,
Like a beloved returning friend
From absence doubly dear.

Wert thou for ever in our sight,
Might we not love thee less ?
But *now* thou bringest new delight,
Thou *still* hast power to bless.

.   .   .   .   .

And still thine exquisite perfume
Is precious as of old ;
And still thy modest tender bloom
It joys me to behold."

Another poet far from the home of his birth thus expresses the delight experienced in finding his favourite flower in the garden of a palace :—

"Sweet tenant of the hedgerow wild,
Whose virgin sigh perfumes the air,
Methinks thy beauty, pure and mild,
Is lost amid yon gay parterre.

Oh ! while thy fragrance I inhale,
Far other scenes before me rise ;
Scenes loved and lost, in vision pale,
They float before my humid eyes.

.

Far o'er the sea, far o'er the sea,
Where milder suns in summer smile,
Exists the land so dear to me,
Beloved England's verdant isle.

There first I knew thee, lowly flower,
In copse remote, so wildly sweet ;
Nor dreamt in pround and foreign bower,
Thy modest form I e'er should greet."

Wordsworth compares the sweetness of a maiden by reference to

> " A Violet by a mossy stone
> Half hidden from the eye,
> Fair as a star, when only one
> Is shining in the sky,"

a most delightful method of conveying the impression he desires to make.

A pleasant retrospect is suggested in the lines by Tennyson :—

> •" The smell of Violets hidden in the green
> Pour'd back into my empty soul and frame
> The times when I remember to have been
> Joyful and free from blame."

Although all these sing of the purple Violet and its delicious fragrance, yet the yellow Violet is not forgotten by one poet.

> " When beechen buds begin to swell,
> And woods the blue-bird's warble know,
> The yellow violet's modest bell
> Peeps from the last year's leaves below.
>
> Ere russet fields their green resume,
> Sweet flower, I love, in forest bare,
> To meet thee, when thy faint perfume
> Alone is in the virgin air.
>
> .   •   •   •   •   •
>
> And when again the genial hour
> Awakes the painted tribes of light,
> I'll not o'erlook the modest flower
> That made the woods of April bright."

As a rule, when speaking of Violets one is apt to think only of the purple-coloured varieties of *Viola odorata*, which we are so accustomed to see in the hedgerow, in our gardens, and on sale in the street ; and to forget the existence of other forms of the Violet, which, if perhaps not so fragrant as that referred to above, are at least interesting and worthy of notice. These remarks do not apply only to the more noteworthy cultivated varieties of white and various shades of blue and purple, but to the wildings both of this country and of other lands. For instance, few people when thinking of Violets call to mind *Viola lutea,* the yellow Violet found on the moorland pastures of Wales and the North Country, or of the still more common *Viola tricolor* or Heart's-ease; but such they are. A list is here appended of some of the most common of these lesser known Violets.

Viola altaica. — Locality, Altaian Mountains. This possesses large yellow flowers. In growth the plant is creeping, and has oval leaves; height about 4 inches. It bears its flowers in April and May. This is one of the varieties from which the garden Pansy and Viola are said to have been derived, by means of various crossings. At any rate, it would make a good stock to work on for further breaks in these flowers.

Viola biflora (Two-flowered yellow Violet).—Found in Europe, Asia, and America. Two very small yellow flowers, streaked with black, are borne on each footstalk. A true alpine, having a creeping habit, enabling it to cover up bare stone work very quickly, making it a most useful plant for the rock garden, where it should grow well.

Viola calcarata (Spurred Violet).—An Alpine Violet much resembling *Viola cornuta* in the shape of its flower, with the long spur or horn characteristic of that species. The growth, however, is quite different, the plant increasing itself by means of runners under the earth. It possesses large purple flowers, which are produced in the greatest profusion, almost concealing the foliage which is very small.

This is another of the supposed parents of the

cultivated garden Pansy and Viola, and a species that has not been much worked by the hybridists.

Viola cornuta (Horned Violet).—This native of the Pyrenees and Alps is probably better known and more commonly grown than any other of these Violets. For many years it has been used in rock gardens and for edgings in the hardy flower garden. Being a first-rate plant for bedding, it is still in great request in parks and other open spaces, for bedding purposes; its sweet-scented flowers of pale blue or white create a most pleasing effect. Of late years, however, it has been giving way to the more varied hues of its progeny—the result of crosses made with the garden pansy—which are now known as Tufted Pansies or Violas.

For hybridising purposes, *Viola cornuta* is invaluable, imparting to its progeny that "tufted root growth which makes the 'Violetta' stain perennial" in no small measure, and it is to this plant and crosses made with it, that we must look for the medium from which we are to get our best Tufted Pansies in the future.

Viola cucullata.—This is a large American Violet much resembling our own common sweet-scented Violet, but the flower lacks the much-desired delicious fragrance. Though now grown as a garden variety, it came in the first place from America, where it is found in all situations, but does best in moist places. The flowers are of a pure purple colour, measuring $1\frac{1}{2}$ inches across, and are borne on very long footstalks some 9 inches in length.

Viola hirta (Hairy Violet).—This species is fairly common in Britain, its habitation being chiefly woods and undergrowths on chalky soil. In appearance it is not unlike *Viola odorata*, with greyish blue flowers streaked with dark lines and having little or no scent. Situation and soil are great factors in its variability.

Viola lutea.—This species is very common on the Welsh and Scotch mountains, growing freely and

AN EXHIBIT OF VIOLET BLOOMS

blossoming profusely amidst the pasture. It possesses large yellow flowers, rayed black. In growth it is very pansy-like and has a fine tufted habit and fibrous root. It is another of the parents of the cultivated Pansy.

Viola odorata (Sweet Violet).—Besides possessing the most delicious scent, this is one of the most common of the Violets, being distributed freely throughout the entire length and breadth of Europe and also in Northern Asia. It will grow almost anywhere, so long as the air is pure and wholesome, and can be naturalised with the greatest facility, the soil best suiting it, however, being a good medium loam. Fog has a most deleterious effect on *Viola odorata* as well as on many other Violets, and for this reason it cannot be grown or do well near large towns where the bad influence of smoke-laden atmosphere is eventually fatal to its growth. In its wild state, there are two varieties, purple and white. Its treatment, together with that of the many varieties originating from it, is discussed fully elsewhere.

Viola palustris (Marsh Violet).—Another fairly common British species. As its name denotes, this is usually found in moist and humid situations, marshes, etc. It is most commonly met with in Yorkshire and elsewhere in the North. The flowers are lilac or white and possess no scent. In growth it is very similar to that of *Viola odorata*.

Viola pedata (Bird's-foot Violet). — An American species of great beauty, bearing flowers measuring an inch across. The flowers vary to great extent, being pale or deep lilac, purple, or blue. The two upper petals are frequently of a velvety texture. The plant takes its name from the shape of the leaves which are deeply divided, giving them an appearance, by no means unlike the foot of a bird.

A rare variety of this is *V. P. bicolor*, which possess

blue and white flowers. This, however, is not so hardy as *V. pedata* and more than ordinary care has to be taken in growing it.

Another rare variety is *V. P. alba* bearing white flowers. *Viola pedata* blossoms in the Summer.

V. sylvestris (Wood Violet).—Another British species with flowers of purplish lilac. Very close growing, with heart-shaped leaves; in height about five inches. Flowers from April to June.

V. tricolor (Heart's-ease).—This is the species around which a very great interest centres, it being commonly understood that from this species the present-day garden Pansy obtained its origin. Apart from this question, it is one of the most familiar of flowers, growing wild throughout the United Kingdom and varying greatly in colour and size. For years it has been grown in the cottage gardens of the countryside, and many and curious are the names which have been bestowed on it by rural admirers. All betoken some pretty fancy or tradition with which the Heart's-ease is associated. Some of them are: Heart's-ease, Three-Faces-under-a-Hood, Forget-me-Not, Herb-Trinity, Love-and-Idleness, Love-in-Idleness, Live-in-Idleness, Call-me-to-you, Cuddle-me-to-you, Jump-up-and-kiss-me, Kiss-me-ere-I-rise, Kiss-me-at-the-Garden-Gate, Tittle-my-Fancy, Pink-of-my-John, Step-mother.

Shakespeare, in " A Midsummer Night's Dream " makes Oberon bid Puck to obtain,

> " A little western flower
> Before milk white, now purple with Love's wound,"
> And maidens call it love-in-idleness.

He says,

> " Fetch me that flower—the herb I showed thee once ;
> The juice of it, on sleeping eyelids laid
> Will make a man or woman madly dote
> Upon the next live creature that it sees."

Viola tricolor derives its common name of Pansy, from the French *pensées*, thoughts.   Ophelia says ·—

> "And there's Pansies—that's for thoughts."

Almost any soil will suit this plant and it is quite at home in the rock garden.

CHAPTER XIV

SWEET VIOLETS

WITH comparatively little trouble Violets may be grown most successfully, and a plentiful supply of flowers obtained, where judicious treatment is accorded the plants.

There are two types of the Sweet Violet, namely, single and double, and it is mainly a matter of taste as to which of the two types is the more pleasing and useful. The single type, however, is somewhat hardier than the double, and is the more suitable for growing in the open during the winter months.

SOIL

Happily, Violets are not particularly fastidious as to the soil they are grown in, although they show their appreciation of thoughtfulness in this respect. Any good garden soil will be found to produce quite satisfactory results. Rank manure, however, is specially unsuited for digging into ground into which Violets are to be planted. Much leaf growth takes place in this event, but the flowers are few and indifferent. Rather do they succeed in ground in which plenty of leaf soil has been incorporated. If the soil be heavy, the incorporation of decaying leaves would be a particularly good way to treat it. Decayed cow manure should also be dug in where the soil happens to be very light and hungry in character.

Violets will do well in ground prepared as advised for growing Pansies and Violas, providing no rank manure be used; and that method of preparation will be found to answer splendidly. The soil between the plants should be constantly stirred by the use of the hoe, and a good mulching given the plants in June.

To obtain the best results, Violets should not be grown in the same soil for more than one season, but should be given fresh quarters every year. The cultivated Violet is one of the first flowers to suffer if in any way neglected, and it is only by a careful and consistent system of cultivation that the best results may be expected to accrue. If left to grow on of their own accord, Violets quickly deteriorate, the foliage becoming matted together and weakly, in consequence of which the plant produces flowers of poor quality, and of these but few.

POSITION

Having regard to the fact that the Violet by nature is fond of the shade, a position in which this may be obtained should be afforded the plants where possible. By *shade*, it is not meant that the plants should be placed in a position where they get no sunshine at all. Rather is it intended to apply to a position where they obtain filtered sunshine such as the shady side of a hedge, rows of peas, etc., or any such semi-shaded position. If planted in quarters where they are likely to obtain a very great amount of sun, and therefore in all probability a dry position, Violets almost invariably become invested with red spider, to which pest these plants are in so great a degree subject.

They may be left in the quarters where they are planted out throughout the winter, evolving their flowers freely far into the Autumn and again during the succeeding Spring; but with comparatively little trouble a continuous succession of bloom may be obtained through out the winter months. For the attainment of this succession of flowers, therefore, it is the practice to grow plants in frames during the winter months.

GROWING IN FRAMES

There are two methods by which the plants may be grown in frames. One is to place a shallow frame around the plants in the beds where they have been growing during the summer; the other method is to lift the plants and place them in a frame, containing a good open soil, during September. The former method, of course, entails less trouble, but by following the latter method better results are more likely to be obtained. The frame in which the plants are to be transplanted should be arranged in a position where it will obtain as much of the sun's warmth as possible during the winter months, as this, of course, is a decided advantage.

If the shading medium which was employed when the plants were growing in their summer quarters can be removed, this does away to a great extent with at any rate one disadvantage attaching to the method of framing the plants as they stand.

As we said before, the frame used should be a shallow one, placed so that the plants are quite close to the frame lights, and it should have a decided slope to the south.

The soil in which the plants are to be transplanted should have plenty of sand and leaf soil intermixed with it, so that it is rendered nice and open. Before lifting the plants from their summer quarters, a thorough watering should be given them, thus allowing for greater facility in lifting them with a good ball of soil and causing less damage to the roots. They should then be transferred to the frame forthwith. When this is done, the plants will soon recover, and in the space of a week or so should have well got hold of the soil in their new quarters. They should be planted firmly, about 8 inches to a foot apart, and a good watering-in given. All dead leaves, etc., should be removed before planting, and the plants should be allowed a little shade for a day or two, in order that they may not wither.

The frame lights should not be put on if the weather remains fairly mild, and in less satisfactory weather as much ventilation as possible should be given night and day. As soon as it becomes frosty, however, the frame-lights should be kept on, and if very severe, mats and boards should be used as a covering and protection, and straw, etc., should be placed round the sides of the frame to keep out the frost.

To water the plants during very severe weather, unless they become very dry—which is most unlikely—is not recommended. Plants lifted very early in September, and treatment accorded them in the manner shown above, should come into bloom during October and should continue so throughout the Winter, and until March is past.

Where the plants are framed as they stand in their summer quarters, it will be found very beneficial to aerate the soil well, and to give a slight mulching with well-decayed manure, as well as a good watering, before closing the frame.

A most important point to remember when growing Violets in frames is, that air should be admitted freely on every possible occasion. If this is not attended to, there is a very grave risk that the plants will suffer from mildew.

In the mild parts of the south, plants grown absolutely in the open will develop their blooms during the winter months quite readily, especially if they be planted in a sheltered position or warm aspect. But, apart from the

G

wild varieties, the cultivated single-flowered kinds are far more suitable for this method of culture, being hardier and stronger growing than the double varieties.

PROPAGATION AND PLANTING OUT

This is best done early in April, when the plants in frames have finished flowering. A number of runners will have emanated from each plant, and to aid these the more quickly to become strongly rooted, some light sandy soil an inch or so deep should be placed amongst the plants. When well rooted, these runners should be separated from the parent plant, when they will be ready to be planted out.

The old clumps of plants themselves may also be pulled to pieces, if a number of plants are desired. Each clump will divide into about half a dozen pieces, more or less; each piece should have three crowns, and should be healthy and possess a fair number of roots. They may be put straight into their summer quarters, or planted out in specially prepared beds in the first instance until they are quite well established plants. There is, however, little, if any, advantage attaching to the latter course of proceedure. The best plan is to rake over the ground in which the runners and tufts are to be grown, and incorporate at the same time a quantity of sand and leaf-soil. The ground in which they are to planted should be dug two spits deep, and a liberal quantity of well-rotted manure and other ingredients, according to the nature of the soil, dug in. A north aspect should be chosen if possible, or at any rate a cool position, as before advised, or in warmer aspects where plenty of shade may be obtained. A distance of about 15 to 18 inches should be left between each plant, and the same space between the rows when planting; but in the case of the single varieties, which

PLANTING VIOLETS FOR MARKET AT MESSRS. ISAAC HOUSE'S NURSERIES, WESTBURY-ON-TRYM

are stronger growing than the double, 2 feet each way will not be too much. Immediately the planting is completed a thorough watering should be given, and the plants should quickly become established.

In dealing with the double varieties, it is advocated by some growers that the best method is to pot up the divided pieces into pots 3 inches in diameter, using a compost consisting of loam, leaf-soil, and sand in about equal quantities. When these pieces have become established and have grown into thoroughly strong plants, plant them out in their summer quarters. It is a question, however, whether there be any real advantage attaching to this method, though in the case of crowns with very few roots there is a better prospect of their rooting quickly and becoming established with more certainty of success. After these growths have been potted up, and having been well watered in, they should be arranged in a sheltered position and shade afforded until established. It should not be long before each piece has become a strong and healthy plant.

General Cultivation during the Summer

Much good may be accomplished by attending to the plants' welfare by the means of watering, hoeing between the rows, and syringing. In dry weather water should be given freely. If the plants are affected by mildew or red spider, a good dusting with sulphur will eliminate the former, and a dressing of lime and soot the latter, repeating the dressing until the pest is eradicated.

No runners should be allowed to grow during the summer months (these are shoots issuing from the "crowns") for they serve only to impoverish the plants, and have the effect of causing them to produce but few flowers, and these of poor quality. These runners, however, instead of being destroyed may be planted in a

G *

shady corner as they are removed, and will grow into nice plants ready for flowering the next season. They should be transplanted in the beds in the autumn, selecting a genial aspect.

Early in June a top dressing or mulching, consisting of well rotted manure incorporating therewith some leaf-soil and road grit, should be placed around the plants. Of great use is the hoe during this period of the plants' growth, both aerating the soil, by means of which healthy plant life is promoted and at the same time keeping down any weeds there may be.

Liquid manure may be applied in the form of cow or horse manure, either of which has been placed in a large vessel of water and soaked for a week or so, being frequently stirred in the interval. This should not be made use of too strong, however, but a very dilute solution used.

The chief points to remember in Violet culture are— primarily, clear atmosphere, Violets being a total failure in and around large towns ; secondly, affording the plants ample shade from the sun during the summer months ; and thirdly, keeping the red spider at bay by means of frequent syringings. The plants must not be allowed to get dry at the roots. These details of treatment should be attended to throughout the summer months, and by September, when the plants are ready for transplanting into frames, or for transferring to large pots, they should be fine, healthy, and well-developed specimens.

PROPAGATION BY SEED

Single Violets may be propagated by means of seed, which may be sown in boxes in October and these placed in a cold frame, or by a mid-August sowing in the open. As soon as the seedings are large enough to handle, they should be pricked off in a sheltered bed, planting them some 2 to 3 inches apart. Here they should remain until they have attained a fair size, and then should be transferred to their flowering quarters. The seedlings may also be potted up into 3-inch pots in February, grown on subsequently in cold frames, and after being hardened off, be planted outdoors in early April. Fine strong plants result from this treatment.

POT CULTURE

The pot culture of Violets is practised by some growers. When the crowns have been broken up, or strong-rooted runners obtained, they are planted in pots containing a compost made up as follows: Two parts loam, one part leaf-soil, and one part road grit. The runners or tufts should be potted up in this early in April, inserting about half a dozen pieces in a 6-inch pot. Care should be taken to see that thorough drainage is provided for, in the shape of crocks and the rougher siftings of the compost. As soon as potted, the plants should be placed in a cold frame, where shade may be afforded, and given a gentle watering. In a month's time they will be ready for placing outdoors. A shady position should be chosen, and the pots should be plunged up to their rims. Here they should remain until September, towards the end of which month they should be removed to the conservatory or cool green house. Water should be given freely as the plants require it, though during the very cold weather it should be applied but sparingly.

CHAPTER XV

SINGLE VIOLETS

VARIETIES

Admiral Avellan.—A well-known Violet of fine colour, being a rich warm purple with a reddish hue. The flowers are large, and most deliciously sweet-scented.

California.—Another well-known variety. An extremely handsome flower of large size, and lovely fragrance. The colour is violet-purple. This is a most useful variety for forcing. Each flower is borne on a long footstalk.

Devoniensis.—This variety is somewhat later than the others, but very free flowering. The colour of the flowers, which are large, is a fine deep blue.

Italia.—A strong growing plant, bearing blooms of a rich deep violet colour

La France.—One of the best single varieties of the colour yet introduced. A plant of robust constitution, bearing its flowers on long erect footstalks. The blooms are of a deep metalic blue colour, and measure over an inch across. This variety is most sweetly fragrant.

Luxonne.—A large dark blue flower, which is borne on long stiff stalks. It is a good hardy variety, and a very profuse bloomer.

Perle Rose.—The colour of the flower of this variety

is a beautiful soft shade of rose. Beautifully sweet scented.

Princess Beatrice.—A later variety, possessing large bright blue flowers. In habit it is somewhat dwarf. A very profuse bloomer.

Princess of Wales.—This variety is held in high esteem by all Violet growers, and thought by some to be the most beautiful single violet in cultivation. The flowers are very large, more so even than *La France*; in colour they are a rich violet-blue. The stalks of this variety are very long, sometimes as much as 12 inches. The fragrance of the flowers is very powerful and delicious, and the plant is, on the whole, a very good variety for forcing. The habit is strong, and the blooms are produced in great profusion.

Princesse De Sumonte.—A very beautiful and fragrant Violet; the colour may be described as a white ground flaked with blue.

Victoria Regina.—A well-known variety, somewhat earlier than most others. It has fine large flowers of a violet-blue colour, and possesses a good strong habit.

Wellsiana.—A large deliciously scented violet of a rich purple colour. Its bears its flowers on long stems.

White Czar.—A good, pure white variety. The plant has a strong habit and is a profuse bloomer.

DOUBLE VIOLETS

VARIETIES

Comte de Brazza.—A well-known pure white variety Very sweetly fragrant and free flowering.

De Parme.—A specially fine violet of a pale lavender-blue shade. Free flowering and most useful for winter-flowering in frames.

King of Violets.—Large flower of an indigo blue tint. A good variety for out-door work.

Lady Hume Campbell.—A fine late variety of vigorous growth, hardy and very free-flowering. The colour of the flowers is pale lavender-blue.

Marie Louise.—One of the best known and most widely grown of the double Violets. The flowers are of a bluish-lavender and white colour and most sweetly scented. This variety and *De Parme* are the two varieties most commonly grown by trade growers and florists.

Mdlle Bertha Barron.—A very fine variety of a beautiful dark purplish-blue colour. It has a strong scent, and is very free flowering.

Mrs J. J. Astor.—A variety of distinct colouring, being of a pink heliotrope hue. It is free flowering in the extreme, and the flowers posess a delicious scent.

Neapolitan.—Another good and well-known winter-flowering variety. The colour is lavender with a white centre. This variety, unfortunately, is not a very strong grower, and requires careful culture, therefore, to obtain good results.

The two foregoing lists comprise the best varieties in cultivation, and those most widely grown.

INDEX

ARTIFICIAL fertilisation, 73, 74.
Autumn planting, 36.

BEDS, 39, 40.
Breeding with *Viola cornuta*, 5.

CHARACTER of soil, 38.
Classification of pansies, 6.
Cross fertilisation, artificial, 73.
—— by insects, 19, 72.
Cutting bed, 28.
Cuttings, 26.
—— compost for, 28.
—— in boxes, 33.
—— insertion of, 31, 33.
—— preparation of, 30.
—— propagation by, 26.
—— taking, 30.
—— types of, 29.

DECORATION with pansies, 62.
Difference between pansy and viola (tufted pansy), 4-6.
Display, early, in frames, 46.
Division of old plants, 33, 34.

EARLY blooms, 35, 37, 46.
Effect, planting for colour, 64.
Exhibiting, 57.
—— methods of, 57, 60, 61.
—— packing blooms for, 57.

FERTILISATION, 5, 72.
—— artificial, 73, 74.
—— by insects, 19.
Flower garden, pansies in the, 64.
Frame, propagating, 28.

Fungoid growth, 54

GAMBIER, Lord, 1.
Greenfly, 25.
Ground, preparing, 40.

HEARTSEASE, 1, 92.
History of the pansy, 1-6.

LEATHER jacket grub, 53.
Lifting young plants, 43, 44.

MILDEW, 54.
Millepede, 53.
Miniature Tufted Pansy (see Violetta), 67.
Mulching, 45, 51.

ORIGIN of the pansy, 1.

PANSIES, 7.
—— general culture of, 51.
—— grown for market, 10.
—— propagation of, by cuttings, 26.
—— —— by division, 33.
—— —— by seed, 18.
Pansy, Continental, 10.
—— fancy, 8.
—— show, 7.
—— tufted (see Tufted Pansy), 11
—— tray, 57, 58.
Planting in beds for exhibition purposes, 40, 42, 43.
—— out, 36, 44.
Plants received from specialist, 45.
Pots, culture in, 47.
Propagation, 18.

Rock garden, violettas in the, 70, 71.
Rose garden, tufted pansies in the, 65.

Seed, 18, 72, 74.
Seedlings in greenhouse, 24.
—— planting, 25, 26.
—— pricking off into boxes, etc., 25.
—— transplanting, 23.
—— treatment of young, 21, 22.
Selections, 76, etc.
Shading, 55, 56.
Slugs, 53.
Soil, 38.
—— for growing pansies in, 38.
—— treatment of, 40, 41, 42.
Sowing seed, 19, 20, 24.
Sports, 74.
Sprays, making up, 58, 59.
Spring planting, 36.
Subsoils, 41.

Thompson, 1.
Treatment of soil, 40, 41, 42.
—— when exhibiting, 54.
Tufted Pansy (a viola), 11.
—— for bedding, 81.
—— for exhibition, 79.
—— miniature (see Violetta), 67.
—— origin of, 6.
—— rayless, 14.
—— shapes of, 12.
Types of pansies, 4, 6.

Varieties, raising new, 72.
Viola (see Tufted Pansy), 11.
Viola altaica, 89.

Viola biflora, 89.
—— *calcarata*, 89.
—— *cornuta*, 67, 90.
—— *cucullata*, 90.
—— *hirta*, 90.
—— *lutea*, 89, 90.
—— *odorata*, 91.
—— *palustris*, 91.
—— *pedata*, 91.
—— *sylvestris*, 92.
—— *tricolor*, 1, 89, 92.
Violet, in Poetry, 86, 87, 88.
—— the, 86.
Violets, by seed, 100.
—— double, 99, 103.
—— general cultivation during summer, 99.
—— growing in frames, 96.
—— in pots, 99.
—— pests of, 99.
—— planting in frames, 96, 97.
—— planting out, 98.
—— position for, 95.
—— pot culture, 101.
—— propagation, 98.
—— sweet, 94.
—— ——, soil for, 94.
—— —— selections, 102, 103.
—— wild, 89.
Violettas, 67.
—— as rock plants, 70, 71.
—— definition of, 68, 69.
—— in baskets, 48.
—— in pans, 49.
—— properties of, 68, 69.
—— selections of the best, 83.
—— the uses of, 70, 71.

Wireworm, 52.

THE COUNTRY HANDBOOKS

An Illustrated Series of Practical Handbooks dealing with Country Life. Suitable for the Pocket or Knapsack

EDITED BY HARRY ROBERTS

Price 3s. net.   Bound in Limp Cloth.
Price 4s. net.   Bound in Limp Leather.

THE TRAMP'S HANDBOOK. By HARRY ROBERTS. With over fifty illustrations by WALTER PASCOE. A volume containing much valuable advice to the amateur gipsy, traveller, or cyclist, as to camping-out, cooking, &c.

THE MOTOR BOOK. By R. T. MECREDY. With numerous illustrations. An invaluable handbook that should find a place in the library of every motorist, or even in the car itself.

THE TREE BOOK. By MARY KNOWLES JARVIS. Containing varied and useful information relating to forests, together with a special chapter on Practical Forestry.

THE STILL ROOM. By Mrs CHARLES ROUNDELL. A book of information upon preserving, pickling, bottling, distilling, &c., with many useful hints upon the dairy.

THE BIRD BOOK. By A. J. R. ROBERTS. A guide to the study of bird life, with hints as to recognising various species by their flight or their note.

THE STABLE HANDBOOK. By T. F. DALE. With numerous illustrations.

THE FISHERMAN'S HANDBOOK. By EDGAR S. SHRUBSOLE. With numerous illustrations and diagrams.

THE SAILING HANDBOOK. By CLOVE HITCH. With numerous illustrations.

THE KENNEL HANDBOOK. By C. J. DAVIES. With numerous illustrations.

THE GUN ROOM. By ALEXANDER INNES SHAND, Author of "Shooting" in "The Haddon Hall" Library. With numerous illustrations.

THE LITTLE FARM. By "HOME COUNTIES." With numerous illustrations.

THE COUNTRY COTTAGE. By G. Ll. MORRIS and E. WOOD.

THE VET. BOOK. By FRANK T. BARTON, M.R.C.V.S

THE INSECT BOOK. By PERCIVAL WESTELL.

THE SMALL HOLDING. By F. E. GREEN.

THE PHOTOGRAPHER'S HANDBOOK. By JAMES DOUGLAS and CHARLES HARRISON.

Handbooks of Practical Gardening

EDITED BY HARRY ROBERTS

Price 2s. 6d. net each. Crown 8vo. Illustrated.

THE BOOK OF ASPARAGUS. With sections on Celery, Salsify, Scorzonera, and Seakale; and a chapter on their cooking and preparation for the table. By CHARLES ILOTT, F.R.H.S., Lecturer on Horticulture to the Cornwall County Council.
"The work of a specialist. Mr Ilott gives us—for a matter of half-a-crown—the ripe experience of a lifetime."—*Speaker.*

THE BOOK OF THE GREENHOUSE. By J. C. TALLACK, F.R.H.S., Head Gardener at Shipley Hall.
"A serviceable handbook for the practical gardener, written with exceptional knowledge of horticultural work."—*Outlook.*

THE BOOK OF THE GRAPE. With a chapter on the History and Decorative Value of the Vines. By H. W. WARD, F.R.H.S., late Head Gardener at Longford Castle.
"A mine of useful information."—*St James's Gazette.*

THE BOOK OF OLD-FASHIONED FLOWERS. By HARRY ROBERTS, Author of "The Chronicle of a Cornish Garden."
"All who wish for a real old-fashioned garden should certainly study this most excellent and practical book."—*Bookman.*

THE BOOK OF BULBS. By S. ARNOTT, F.R.H.S., of Carsethorne, near Dumfries. Together with an introductory chapter on the Botany of Bulbs by the Editor.
"Skilled and instructive. It notably enriches the series in which it appears."—*Scotsman.*

THE BOOK OF THE APPLE. By H. H. THOMAS, Assistant Editor of *The Garden,* late of the Royal Gardens, Windsor. Together with chapters by the Editor on the History and Cooking of the Apple and the Preparation of Cider.
"This is a most useful volume, which every grower, whether for his own use or for the market, should consult."—*Spectator.*

THE BOOK OF VEGETABLES. By GEORGE WYTHES, V.M.H., Head Gardener to the Duke of Northumberland. Together with chapters on the History and Cookery of Vegetables by the Editor.
"Thoroughly practical. The book can be highly recommended."—*Morning Post.*

THE BOOK OF ORCHIDS. By W. H. WHITE, F.R.H.S., Orchid Grower to Sir Trevor Lawrence, President of the Royal Horticultural Society.
"There are few writers so well qualified to write with authority upon these flowers."—*Scotsman.*

THE BOOK OF THE STRAWBERRY. With chapters on the Raspberry, Blackberry, Loganberry, Japanese Wineberry, and Allied Fruits. By EDWIN BECKETT, F.R.H.S.
"Mr Beckett deals with his subject in a thorough practical manner . . . and fully maintains the general excellence shown in the previous volumes of this series."—*Morning Post.*

THE BOOK OF CLIMBING PLANTS. By S. ARNOTT, F.R.H.S., Author of "The Book of Bulbs."
"This is a concise, practical, and well-informed exposition of skilled knowledge as to the training of creepers, &c."—*Scotsman.*

THE BOOK OF PEARS AND PLUMS.
By the Rev. E. BARTRUM, D.D., F.R.H.S.
"The writer knows as much about the growing of Pears and Plums as Dean Hole knows about the cultivation of Roses."—*Scotsman.*

THE BOOK OF HERBS. By LADY ROSALIND NORTHCOTE.

THE BOOK OF THE WILD GARDEN.
By S. W. FITZHERBERT.

THE BOOK OF THE HONEY-BEE.
By CHARLES HARRISON.

THE BOOK OF SHRUBS. By GEORGE GORDON, V.M.H.,
Editor of *The Gardener's Magazine.*
A special feature of this book lies in the distinction which it makes between shrubs and trees peculiarly suited to garden cultivation, and those appropriate to the park and woodland. The author desires to encourage the culture of shrubs in gardens, and indicates those most suit. able for various purposes and situations.

THE BOOK OF THE DAFFODIL.
By the Rev. S. EUGENE BOURNE.
The author supplies valuable information on the cultivation of daffodils gained by the results of his own personal experience.

THE BOOK OF THE LILY. By W. GOLDRING.
A description of, and a practical guide to, the cultivation of all the lilies usually to be found in British gardens.

THE BOOK OF TOPIARY. By CHARLES H. CURTIS
and W. GIBSON, Head Gardener at Levens Hall.
A textbook of the topiary art, together with some account and famous examples of the application of that art.

THE BOOK OF TOWN AND WINDOW GARDENING.
By Mrs F. A. BARDSWELL.

THE BOOK OF RARER VEGETABLES. By GEORGE
WYTHES, V.M.H., Head Gardener to the Duke of Northumberland, and HARRY ROBERTS.

THE BOOK OF THE IRIS. By R. IRWIN LYNCH, A.L.S.,
Curator of the Botanic Gardens, Cambridge.

THE BOOK OF GARDEN FURNITURE.
By CHARLES THONGER.

THE BOOK OF THE CARNATION.
By C. P. BROTHERSTON and MARTIN R. SMITH.

THE BOOK OF THE SCENTED GARDEN.
By F. W. BURBIDGE, M.A., V.M.H., F.R.H.S., London.

THE BOOK OF GARDEN DESIGN.
By CHARLES THONGER.

THE BOOK OF THE WINTER GARDEN.
By D. S. FISH, of the Royal Botanic Gardens, Edinburgh.

THE BOOK OF MARKET GARDENING. By R. LEWIS
CASTLE, Author of "Commercial Fruit Growing, and Grading and Packing of Fruits and Vegetables," &c.

THE BOOK OF ROCK AND WATER GARDENS.
By CHARLES THONGER, Author of "The Book of Garden Design."
A handbook to rock, wall, and water gardening, with a detailed account of the culture of Alpine plants.

THE BOOK OF THE CHRYSANTHEMUM. By PERCY
S. FOLLWILL, Head Gardener at Drumpellier Gardens, Coatbridge.

THE BOOK OF FRUIT BOTTLING.
By EDITH BRADLEY and MAY CROOKE.

THE BOOK OF GARDEN PESTS AND PLANT
DISEASES. By R. HOOPER PEARSON, F.R.H.S.

Printed in Great Britain
by Amazon

41653303R00092